Historic

Maritime Maps

1290-1699

Author: Donald Wigal

Page 4-5:
Map of the most principal maritime explorations

Designed by:
Baseline Co Ltd
127-129 A Nguyen Hue
Fiditourist, 3rd Floor
District 1, Ho Chi Minh City
Vietnam

© 2006, Sirrocco, London, UK
© 2006, Confidential Concepts, Worldwide, USA

Published in 2006 by Grange Books
an imprint of Grange Books Plc
The Grange Kingsnorth Industrial Estate
Hoo, nr Rochester, Kent ME3 9ND
www.grangebooks.co.uk

ISBN 10: 1-84013-925-0
ISBN 13: 978-1-84013-925-9

Printed in China

God said, "Let the waters under heaven come together into a single mass, and let dry land appear". And so it was.
God called the dry land "earth" and the mass of waters "seas", and God saw that it was good.

— Genesis 1: 9-10 (10th century B.C)

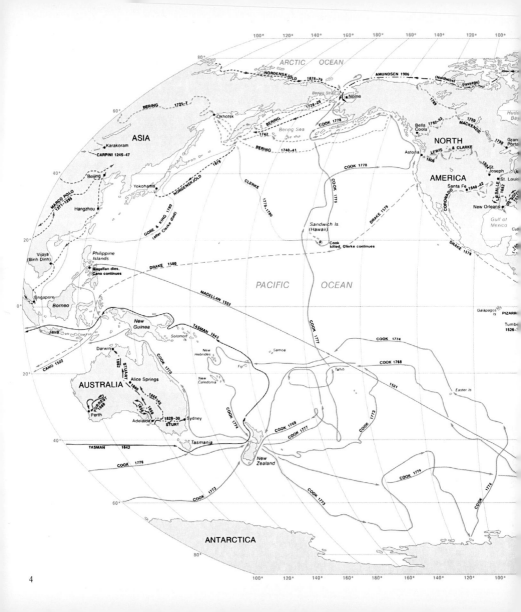

4

Greenland

Iceland

NORDENSKJOLD 1878-79

Novaya
Zemlya

Tromsø

BERING 1725-7

Oslo

St
Petersburg

ASIA

HUDSON 1610

AMUNDSEN 1903

LEIF ERIKSSON 1001

CABOT 1497

Kiev

CARPINI 1245-7

Bristol
London
Plymouth

EUROPE

CABOT 1497

CHAMPLAIN 1604-1616

COOK 1771

Venice

Lyon

Constantinople

MARCO POLO 1271-1295

VERRAZANO 1524

Azores

DA GAMA
1499

Lisbon
Seville

Tabriz

Bahama

COLUMBUS 1493

COLUMBUS 1504

COLUMBUS 1496

Tangier

Tripoli

Mediterranean

Hormuz

Broach

Hispaniola

COLUMBUS 1492-3

CAILLE 1827

BARTH

Canary

Timbuktu

1828

MARCO POLO 1271-1295

COLUMBUS 1493-6
1502-4

Cape Verde

CANO
1522

Kukawa

Galicut

ARABIAN
SEA

COLUMBUS 1498

DIAS 1487

1887-1889

Sumatra

ORELLANA 1541-3

DIAS 1487

AFRICA

STANLEY

1871

Mombasa
Bagamoyo

INDIAN
OCEAN

COOK 1770

Cuzco

SOUTH
AMERICA

DRAKE 1577

COOK 1772-71

MAGELLAN 1519

VASCO DA GAMA 1497

COOK 1772

VASCO DA GAMA 1498

Luanda

DRAKE 1580

DIAS

LIVINGSTONE

1866

1868-1865

VASCO DA GAMA 1498

VASCO DA GAMA 1499

TASMAN 1642

COOK 1770

VALDIVIA 1540-7

Rio de Janeiro

COOK 1776

GORE & KING 1780

DA GAMA 1499

Mauritius

1780

DRAKE 1580

GORE & KING 1780

Valparaiso
Santiago
Buenos Aires

LIVINGSTONE
1841
1847
1853?

Capetown

CANO 1522

COOK 1776

TASMAN 1642

Falkland
Is

ATLANTIC

OCEAN

South Georgia

COOK 1774

COOK 1772

Kerguelen
Is

COOK 1772

Cape Horn

COOK 1776

ANTARCTICA

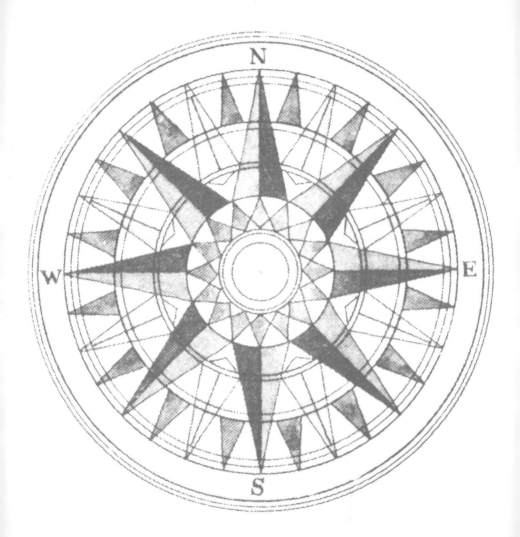

Chronology

About 981:	The Viking, Eric the Red, discovers Greenland.
About 1000:	Leif Ericsson, nephew of Eric the Red, discovers Vinland, later to be known as North America.
1271-95:	Journeys of the Venetian, Marco Polo, in China.
1434:	Gil Eanes, from Portugal, crosses Cape Bojador (The North West Coast of Africa, just south of the Canary Islands).
1427:	The Portuguese discover the Azores.
1489:	Bartholomeu Dias, from Portugal, becomes the first European to cross the Cape of Good Hope successfully.
1492:	Christopher Columbus, from Spain, discovers America.
1497:	Jean Cabot, from Italy, lands on the coast of North America, in a place that will be later called the New Land.
1497:	Vasco da Gama, from Portugal, returns to India by sea, passing by the Cape of Good Hope.
1513:	(17th September) Vasco de Balboa, from Spain, becomes the first European to see the Pacific Ocean while leaving America.
1520-22:	Fernand de Magellan, from Portugal, crosses through, what will later be known as the Straits of Magellan and carries out the first circumnavigation of the world.
1535:	(10th August, St Lawrence Day) Jacques Cartier, from France, reaches Canada.
1610-11:	Henry Hudson, from England, while searching for the North West passage toward the Pacific Ocean discovers Hudson's Bay.
1642:	Abel Janszoon Tamsan, from Holland, famous for the discovery of the Island of Tasmania, discovers New Zealand, Tonga and the Islands of Fiji.
1728:	Vetus Bering, from Denmark, crosses the Strait that separates the countries, later named Eastern Siberia and Alaska.
1768-71, 1772-73 and 1776-79:	James Cook, from England, explores the Islands of the Southern Oceans three times.
1829-33:	John Ross, from England, and his nephew James discover the magnetic North Pole on the Island of Somerset.
1820:	The American, Nathaniel Palmer, becomes the first European to have seen the Antarctic.
1838:	The American, Charles Wilkes, discovers Wilkes Land.
1886:	The American, Robert Peary, explores the ice sheet of Greenland.
1906:	Roald Amundsen, from Norway, becomes the first man to reach the South Pole.
1908:	The American, Vilhjalmur Stefansson explores the Canadian Arctic.
1909:	The American, Matthew Henson, plants the American flag near the North Pole.
1914:	The American, Robert Bartlett, reaches Siberia.
1956:	Final expedition of the American Richard Byrd in the Arctic.

Maps, even those dating from centuries ago, constantly influence our daily lives. They are one of the things which are part of our daily environment. Throughout history, besides having a utilitarian function, every single map symbolizes the period of time in which it was created. We are often reminded of the romance of antique maritime maps as we see them displayed in museums, or reproductions of them framed on the walls of private houses or institutions. In a Vermeer painting a map may be seen telling a story-within-a-story. In plays and films maps typically set the period.

The Artist's Studio

Johannes Vermeer van Delft (1632-1675), c. 1665
Oil on canvas, 120 x 100 cm
Kunsthistorisches Museum, Vienna

In fiction they may be called on to remind the reader of a world beyond the story's setting (in Herman Melville's Moby Dick, for example). Each map is, therefore, a priceless snapshot in the on-going album of humankind. This is especially true with antique maps where we can see the world through the eyes of our forebears.

While the map maker's vision might later prove to be inadequate, or even incorrect, the unique truth is that his map expresses a story that might not be revealed in any other way. It may well be said that each map maker has effectively traveled in his mind vicariously not only to the envisioned places, but also to the future.

Arab map featuring Arabia as the centre of the world Al-Istakhri

10th century
National Library, Cairo

الحزه سلداى يوے يكدن على ساحله الاوجه الى ازا يفصل بطرطوسه الى بلاد الملطس

وممتد على بلاد اى بوه علیم مه لا ا ترجى وادى الصبن یبرزه جبل طارف

ثم ممتد على البحر المحیط الى سرس ارو اربلاد ملم الى البحر سلوان نجلاسا رمن

البصره على الساحل جى يعود الى المحاد بوه من ارض الاملس جى الخلج ان يعبه هزا الوخلطا

امكذع

One such visionary monk was the 15th century map maker, Fra Mauro. He was certainly responsible for bringing to light the work of several other map makers. In doing so he helped make the transition from the Dark Ages to the beginning of the modern era (c. 1450). Mauro was part of the generation that was at work during the very focus of these significant times, over thirty years before the famous voyage of Christopher Columbus to the New World in 1492.

World Map

---

after 1262
in Psalter Map Manuscript, London, Ms-Add 28681
British Library, London

13

Mauro probably went largely unnoticed in his monastery on an island within the Laguna Veneta (the lagoon that surrounds Venice). But his new map was destined to demand attention. It was large and round – which was unusual – almost two metres (six feet) in diameter, yet still very definitely a map and not a global representation. Most of all, he no longer showed Jerusalem as the center of the world.

For the Asian part of the map Mauro took his data from the writings of Marco Polo. The rest was based on Ptolemy, or his own contemporary sea-faring charts. Mauro's extraordinary work was completed in 1459.

The Pisana map

Unknown Artist, 1290
Parchment, 50 x 105 cm
Bibliothèque nationale de France, Paris

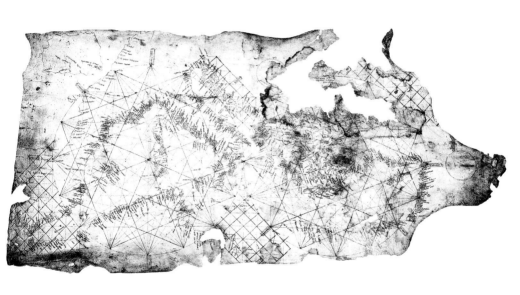

Also in transition was the Earth itself, as after all, its surface was being 'discovered'. Its face was also becoming more clearly defined with each new exploration and subsequent map revision.

Just twenty years before Mauro's map – as if anticipating the need to get such priceless information to the world – Gutenberg (1400-1468) developed his revolutionary printing press. The first printed map in 1477 followed the first printed Bible in 1440. Both were documents that would support, in very distinct ways, the emergence of international humanism.

Atlas (Black Sea)
———————
Petrus Vesconte, 1313
Parchment, 48 x 40 cm
Bibliothèque nationale de France, Paris

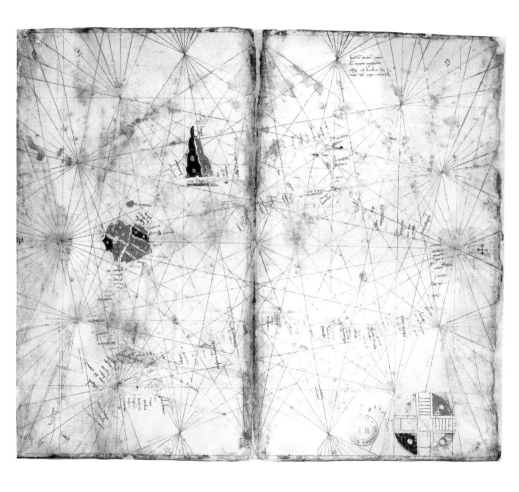

17

The Beginnings of Exploration: 300 BC – 1000 AD

Alexander the Great

During Alexander's triumphant thirteen-year campaign of territorial expansion which began in 336 BC, he extended his empire from Macedonia to India and along the Mediterranean coast southward to Egypt. Although his route of conquest was predominantly by land, he did assign a fleet of ships under his officer, Nearchus, to scout the northern coast of the Indian Ocean towards the Persian/Arabian Gulf.

Atlas (Central Mediterranean Sea)

Petrus Vesconte, 1313
Parchment, 48 x 40 cm
Bibliothèque nationale de France, Paris

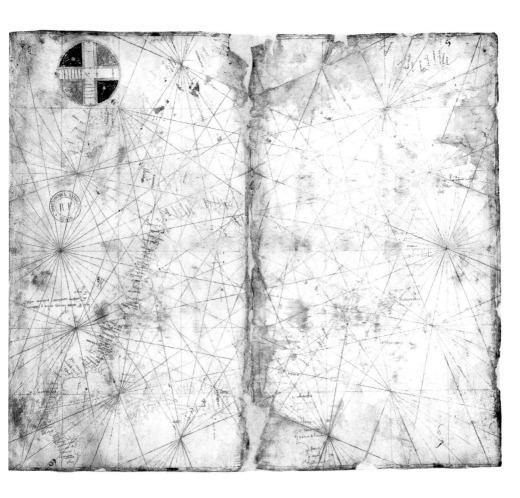

19

Nearchus' coastal exploration, while limited, most likely contributed data that would eventually be used in the preparation of the coastal maps of the area.

Alexander was a military genius who used every opportunity to expand his territory by conquering everything in his path and his western expansion undoubtedly spread Greek culture into Asia. It prepared that part of the world for the concept of obedience to a single King of a universal kingdom on which the Romans would build for political gain.

Atlas (Aegean Sea and Crete)
***

Petrus Vesconte, 1313
Parchment, 48 x 40 cm
Bibliothèque nationale de France, Paris

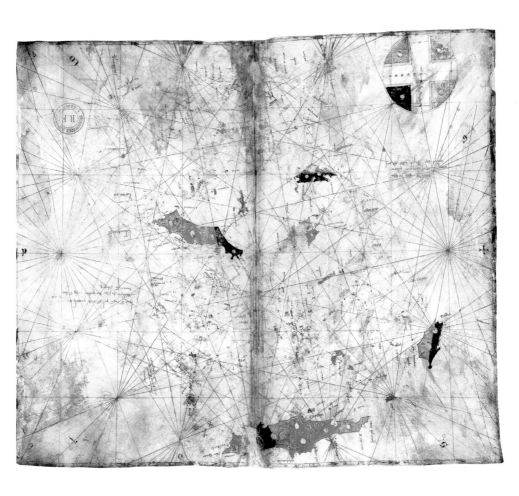

21

Erik the Red (c. 950-1007)

A thousand years ago, the Scandinavian explorers known as the Vikings undertook many journeys and some came to North America to escape the political unrest in Norway. Erik the Red, a descendant of Viking chieftains, established the first European settlement in North America.

Around 981, he and his fleet of twenty five ships discovered the land he named Greenland. About twenty years later, Leif Eriksson (Erik's son), most notable of all the Vikings, discovered Vinland, later to be recognized as North America.

Atlas (Spanish coasts)

Petrus Vesconte, c. 1321
Parchment stuck onto wood, 14.3 x 29.2 cm
Bibliothèque municipale, Lyon

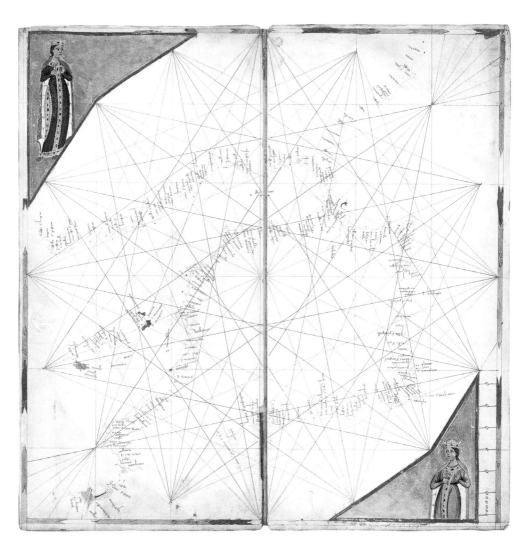

23

Leif Eriksson (c. 970-1020)

In his Saga of Erik the Red, Ericsson records the contemporary accounts of the grandson of one of the earliest colonists of Greenland. The description of the coastline may well constitute the beginning of the first portolano of North America. A collection of sagas known as The Hauksbók and a section of another called The Flateyjarbók are cited as additional evidence, but it has to be admitted that these resources are mixtures of fact and fiction.

Atlas (French, English and Irish Coasts)

Petrus Vesconte, c. 1321
Parchment stuck onto wood, 14.3 x 29.2 cm
Bibliothèque municipale, Lyon

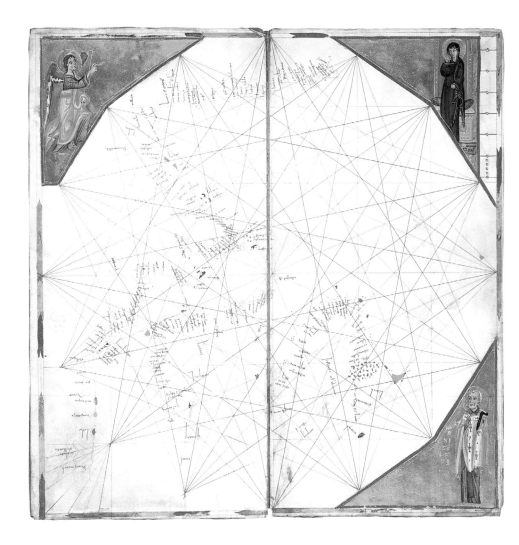

25

We see a similar mixture again in the writings of Marco Polo, Columbus, and other explorers whose enthusiasm often influenced their documentation. Such imagination influenced their maps in general. For example, there are some unicorn-like figures indicating imaginatively weird native animals in a map within the portolano of the St Lawrence Bay area between 1536 and 1542 by Pierre Desceliers.

From the Baltic Sea to the Red Sea

Angelino Dulcert, 1339
Parchment, 75 x 102 cm
Bibliothèque nationale de France, Paris

27

Coming out of the Dark: 1000-1400

Marco Polo (1254-1324)

Every textbook of world history mentions the Venetian, Marco Polo, and his amazing 14th century travels in China. It is quite possible, however, that he never visited Asia at all. The accounts of his travels attributed to him may be simply very clever fiction. But it is more likely that when he was seventeen, Polo did indeed accompany his grandfather and uncle, successful jewel-merchants, on their second trading journey to China during the last quarter of the 13th century. While in prison, Polo apparently related the details of his journeys to a fellow prisoner,

Marco Polo
———
1857
Engraving
Centre historique des Archives nationales, Paris

who conveniently happened to be a popular writer of romantic fiction. Even map makers, whom we might expect to be scientific as much as artistic, incorporated imaginary figures into their work, as seen in several maps here reproduced. These maps often exhibit truly vivid imaginations together with genuine data from scientific exploration. A serious study of them requires a specialized glossary and a knowledge of the history of their time. The first expression of Polo's journey in map form came after his death (1324) in the Catalan Atlas (1375). Many of the places named of the legend in that atlas appear previously only in Polo's descriptions.

World Map (detail)

Abraham Cresques, 1375
in Atlas Catalan, folio V, RC-B-18153
Bibliothèque nationale de France, Paris

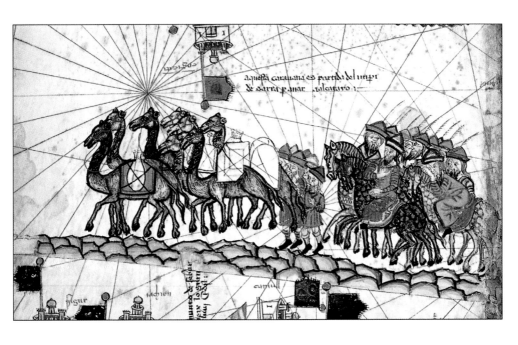

The Franciscans

Two well traveled Franciscan friars – Joannes de Plano Carpini in 1245 and William of Rubruquis in 1253 – were notable among the influential clergy. Their tales were less fanciful than those of Polo, but were often just as outlandish.

The memoirs of other Franciscan missionaries (Giovanni di Monte Corvino in 1294 and Odoric of Pordenone in 1318) supplemented the descriptions of China by Marco Polo. Monte Corvino was the first to report the monsoon cycles that were later vital to understanding sea routes to India.

Marco Polo leaves Venice
on his famous journey to the Far East

in Roman d'Alexandre
Bodleian Library, Oxford

Henry the Navigator (1394-1460)

Seventy years after the death of Marco Polo, a Portuguese Prince was born who would become even more instrumental than the Polos in advancing the Age of Discovery. He would become the 15th century's leading promoter of exploration and the study of geography. Although the Prince came to be known as Henry the Navigator, he did not actually do any navigating on the pioneering Portuguese explorations along the coast of West Africa for which he gained his renown. After a decade of attempts by others, one of Henry's navigators, Gil Eanes, finally rounded Cape Bojador (on the North West African coast just south of the Canary Islands) in 1434.

Catalan Atlas
(Atlantic Ocean and western Mediterranean Sea)

Abraham Cresques, c. 1375
Parchment on wood tablets, 64 x 25 cm
Bibliothèque nationale de France, Paris

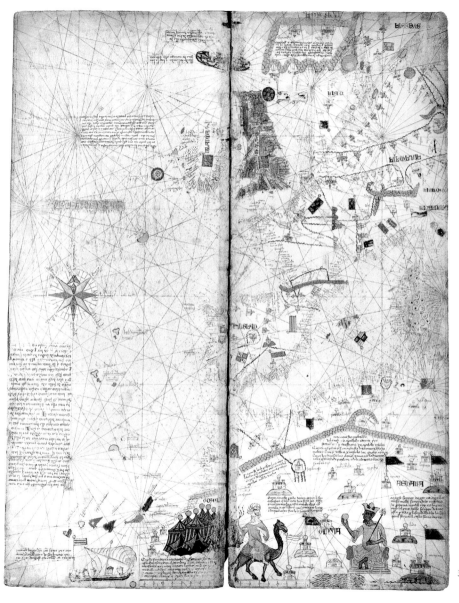

35

It was an area that was seen – mainly because of superstition – as a major obstacle between Europe and the Indies. In fact, Henry apparently told Eanes to either push beyond that point this time or to not return. Of course it was to prove to be only an early hurdle in a much longer journey, but new information from his trip was incorporated into maps by Grazioso Benincasa in 1467 (Maps p. 55 and 57).

About five years later the Portuguese colonized the Azores, which they had discovered in 1427. Expeditions then continued along the coast, mapping the West African coast down to present day Sierra Leone.

Mediterranean Sea

Guillelmus Solieri, c. 1385
Paper, 102 x 65 cm
Bibliothèque nationale de France, Paris

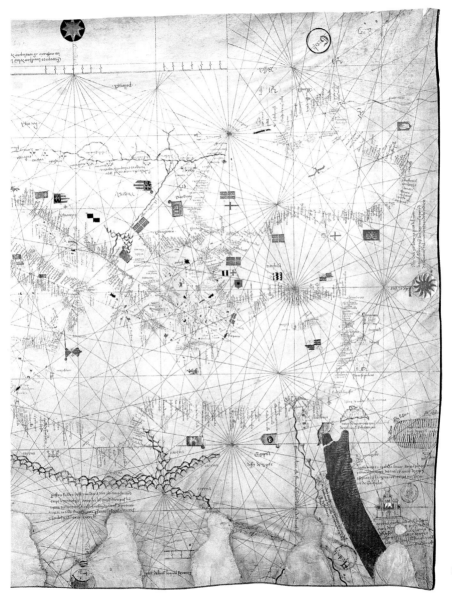

Portolani During this Period

The Pisana School
The Pisana (Map p. 15) is the earliest example (1250-1296) of a portolano. It is the oldest Western navigation map, and as an extremely early (and well known) map which influenced all subsequent maps, especially those of the Catalana and Genovese schools. Although it may have been drawn up in Genoa, it is referred to as the Pisana map because it belonged to a well established family in Pisa during the 19th century. It depicts the Mediterranean Sea in correct proportions.

Venetian Atlas (Western Mediterranean Basin, Portugal, Spain and Western France)

Unknown Artist, c. 1390
Parchment on wood, 23.5 x 15.5 cm
Bibliothèque municipale, Lyon

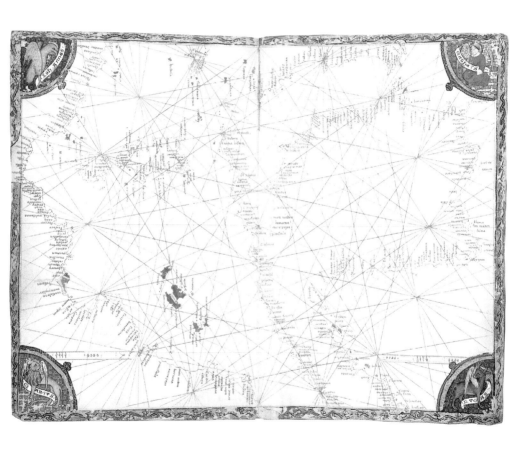

39

The Early Genovese School

The portolani of the Genovese School (1300-1588) in this presentation (Maps p. 17, 19, 21, 23 and 25) were directly influenced by the pioneering 13th century work. In turn they substantially influenced the 14th century Viennese and 16th century Portuguese, Spanish and Italian schools. The corners of Maps 5 and 6 are decorated with popular patron saints of Venice, including St Nicholas and St Lucia. Two anonymous Genovese maps of around 1500 (Maps p. 65 and 67) were drawn by the same map maker using inks similar to those used by the Japanese at about the same time.

Mediterranean Sea and Black Sea

Albertin de Virga, 1409
Parchment, 68 x 43 cm
Bibliothèque nationale de France, Paris

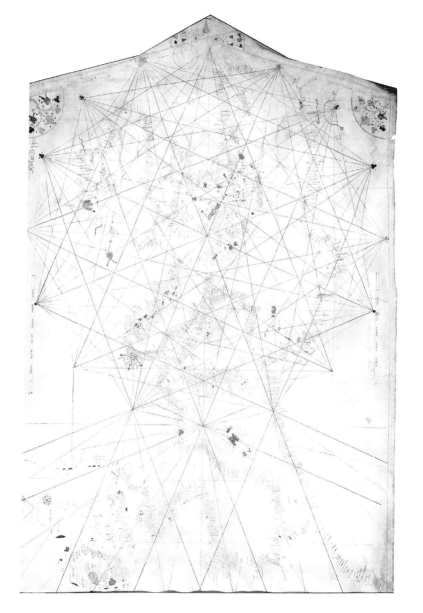

41

The peninsular coasts from Vlorë (Valona) in Albania to the Pagasitikós Gulf in Thessalia are represented in the unfinished map of the Greek coasts (Map p. 65). In the other map (Map p. 67) the coastlines of the Aegean archipelago are shown. It is oriented to the North West, showing a new awareness of magnetic north. The Map seen on p. 69 is known as Cantino's Planisphere (1502), one of the earliest examples of Portuguese maritime cartography. It represents the whole of the known world at the time, including recent Portuguese discoveries of up to 1502.

From the Baltic Sea to the Niger

Mecia de Viladestes, 1413
Parchment, 85 x 115 cm
Bibliothèque nationale de France, Paris

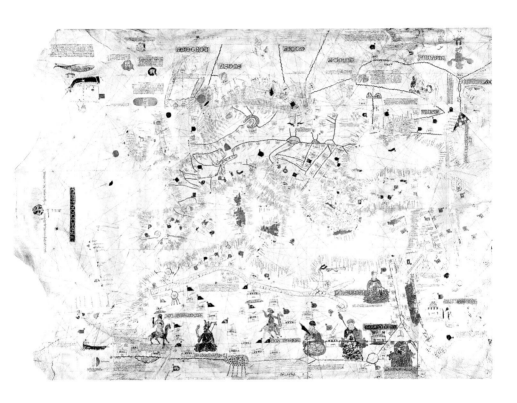

43

The design was influenced by the miniature painters Alexander Bening and Guillaume Vrelant. The large maritime planisphere of Genoan cartographer Nicolaus de Caverio (Map p. 73) bears comparison with Cantino's Planisphere (Map p. 69). It features nomenclature in Portuguese. However, it does not include information from discoveries after 1504. Its graduated latitude scale is an innovation not seen in maps before the 16th century. It is a highly derivative work.

Liber Insularium Archipelagi (Corfu)

Christoforo Buondelmonte, 1420
Coloured paper, 29.5 x 20.5 cm
Bibliothèque nationale de France, Paris

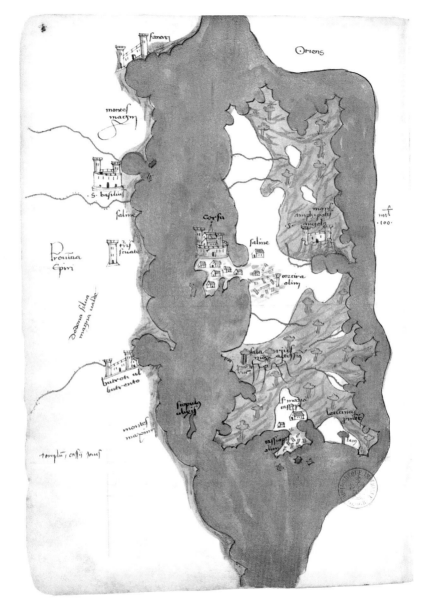

Oriens

fanar

montes
marim

S. basilius

falme

Prouina
Epiri

Corsu

falme

mons
amphipoli
angelo

mf
.100.

grif
sinate

Dodona filia
magna ualde

orira
olim

butroti ul
butrento

sala grif
moy alassio

supuli
ulixis

fmagic
nassi

leucania
ribot

montes
marim

cassiop
olim

las

templũ casfi louis

The same design and nomenclature are seen in the work at Saint Dié of Waldseemüller who was responsible for the first oceanic map in the extremely influential 1513 edition of Ptolemy's Geographia. The Caverio Planisphere outlines the shape of the Indian subcontinent correctly, but does not feature the Red Sea or the Persian/Arabian Gulf – areas the Portuguese had yet to visit.

Liber Insularium Archipelagi (Chios)

Cristoforo Buondelmonte, 1420
Coloured Paper, 29.5 x 20.5 cm
Bibliothèque nationale de France, Paris

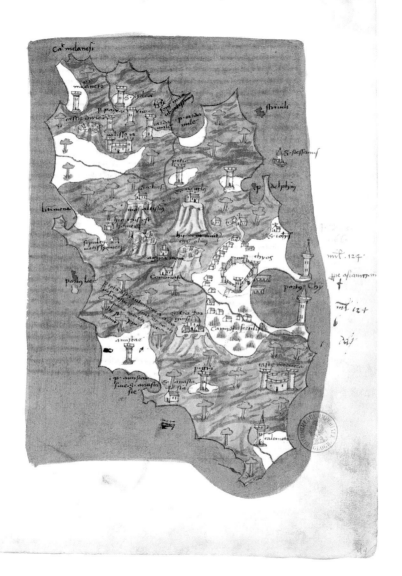

The Catalana School

Early portolani (Maps p. 27, 35, 37, 43, 51 and 53) of the Catalana School in Majorca (c. 1290-1330) also exhibit the long-lasting influence of The Pisana (Map p. 15). Even later examples (Maps, p. 149, 153, 155 and 163) of as late as 1649 also influenced the Portugese, Italian and Spanish schools from the 15th century onwards, as well as the Messina School of the mid 16th to late 17th centuries.

A synthesis of the whole known world is attempted in the Map on p. 27. Unlike previous maps in this collection, the nomenclature inland is important. On the map a region named Terra Nigrorum occurs in the south of Africa.

Mediterranean Sea

Jacobus de Giroldis, 1422
Parchment, 88 x 51 cm
Bibliothèque nationale de France, Paris

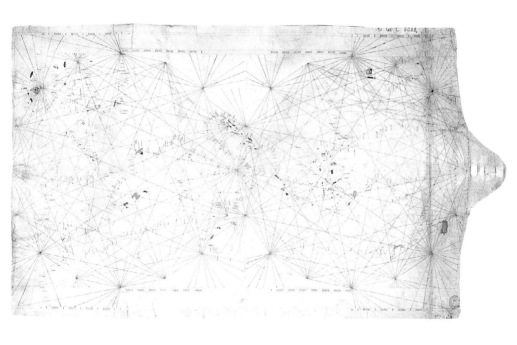

In Asia, the Caspian Sea (Mare de Bacusive Capium) is named. Three of the Canary Islands are specified for the first time. The Majorcan school, of which this map is typical, was to be imitated for centuries.

The Map on p. 35 may have belonged to King Charles V of France, possibly as a gift to him from King John I of Aragon.

In the Map on p. 37, the cartographer indicates in Latin that Europe is 'where Christians live'. Biblical sites and pilgrimage destinations are indicated, including the Holy Sepulchre (the traditional location of Jesus' entombment), St Catherine's Monastery on Mount Sinai, and Mecca.

Mediterranean Sea and Black Sea

Gabriel de Vallsecha, 1447
Parchment, 58 x 93 cm
Bibliothèque nationale de France, Paris

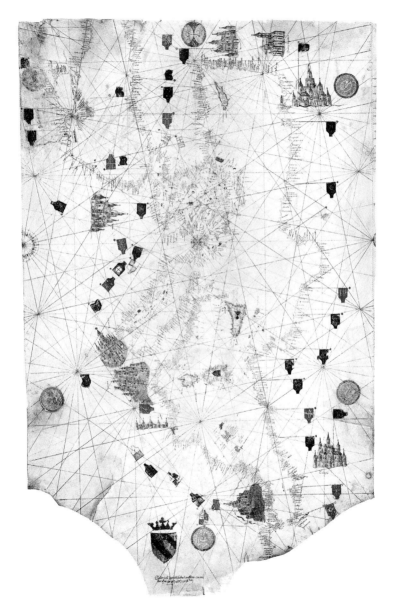

51

The emblem of the Cornaro family, a contemporarily renowned clan, is shown in the Map on p. 39. Some coasts are drawn disproportionately close to each other. The symbols of the four New Testament evangelists feature in the corners (clockwise from the upper right, Matthew is symbolized by a man, Luke by the winged ox, Mark by the winged lion, and John by the eagle). Some important African warlords are represented. One of the ships near the African coast is that of the 14th century Aragonese pirate Jacme Ferrer, who is represented also by a ship in the Map on p. 35.

Atlantic Ocean, Mediterranean Sea and Black Sea

Petrus Roselli, 1462
Parchment, 53 x 83 cm
Bibliothèque nationale de France, Paris

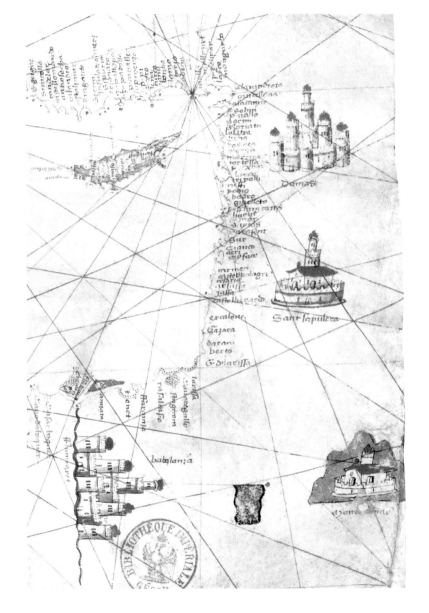

53

Sites are indicated where Arabian sources claimed gold was to be found. That sort of information was usually closely guarded by merchants. The impressive quantity of Joan Martines' output is seen again (p. 149) with his twenty one parchment sheets that make up the Atlas dated 1587 (Maps, p. 153 and 155). His main source seems to have been the 1569 world map of Gerardus Mercator. This is a compilation of nineteen maps. The maps may have been commissioned or intended for use by King Philip II of Spain who at the time was preparing an armada against England. It is Philip's court of arms shown on the map.

Atlas (Atlantic Ocean from Spain to Cape Verde)

Grazioso Benincasa, 1467
Parchment stuck on card, 34.9 x 44.2 cm
Bibliothèque nationale de France, Paris

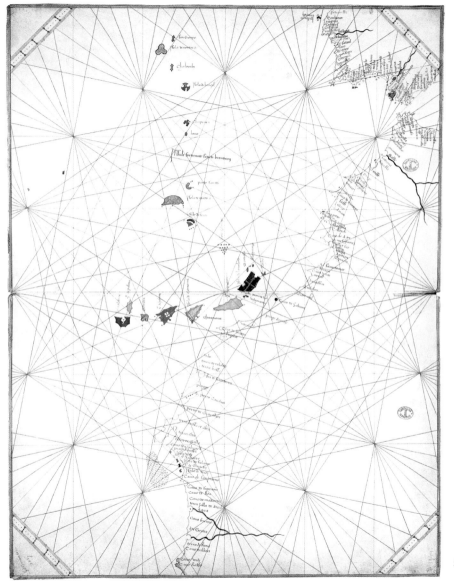

55

The Viennese School

The portolani of the Viennese school (1567-1690) presented here (Maps, p. 39, 41, 49, 55, 57, and 179) shows the influence of the Genovese school. Their own unmistakable influence was primarily on the Spanish school, the Barbary Coast school in Istanbul and the Marseille school.

A close examination of the Map on p. 41 reveals that the artist sketched the outline with a dry point before drawing in the final version. The Black Sea is conveniently reduced in size so as to fit within the allotted space.

Atlas (Atlantic Ocean, from Denmark to Malaga)

Grazioso Benincasa, 1467
Parchment stuck on card, 34.9 x 44.2 cm
Bibliothèque nationale de France, Paris

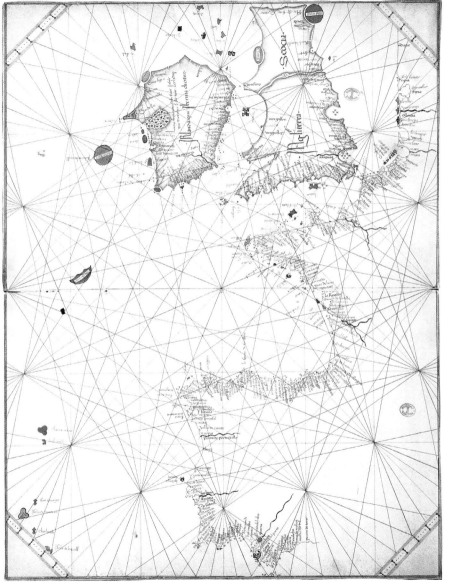

57

The French coastline is somewhat cursorily dealt with, whereas the coasts of England are delineated in some detail. The map maker endeavors to make light of such inconsistencies by presenting three different scales against which to estimate distance.

Symbols that were standard in medieval iconography are used in the Map on p. 49, including the red cross for shallows or sandbanks, and blue lines for lateral cordons. As a young man in the mid 15th century, Grazioso Benincasa kept a diary of his trips sailing across the Mediterranean and Black Seas.

Globe

Martin Behaim, 1492 (1847, copy)
Parchment, stuck on globe of 50.7 cm diameter
Bibliothèque nationale de France, Paris

After losing his ship to pirates, he became a cartographer famous for producing more than twenty two works between 1461 and 1482. We noted above that details of Africa included in this atlas had only recently become known following the return of the explorer navigator Gil Eanes. Yet in 1467 Benincasa was apparently quite prepared to use out of date information for the maps of northern Europe in his atlas, in which he included Maps, p. 55 and 57. A cartographer of the Dutch East India Company, Hessel Gerritsz drew up his map of the Pacific (Map, p. 181) in 1622.

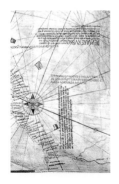

The 'Christopher Columbus' Map

---

c. 1492
Parchment, 70 x 110 cm
Bibliothèque nationale de France, Paris

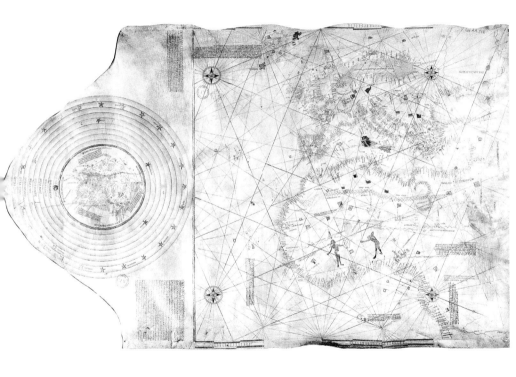

All the recent discoveries are noted, along with unique artistic tributes to Vasco de Balboa, Ferdinand Magellan and Jakob Lemaire. A world map, though very small, is also featured.

Because of its importance to the area, the Aegean Sea was often depicted disproportionately large in maps of the Middle Ages. The whole of the map produced in 1603 by Alvise Gramolin (Map, p. 179) is devoted to the sea and its coastline. All the flags and shields show the crescent moon from Muslim and Ottoman iconography, for the archipelago was under Turkish influence at the time.

World Map

Juan de la Cosa, 1500
Parchment, 95.5 x 177 cm
Museo Naval de Madrid, Madrid

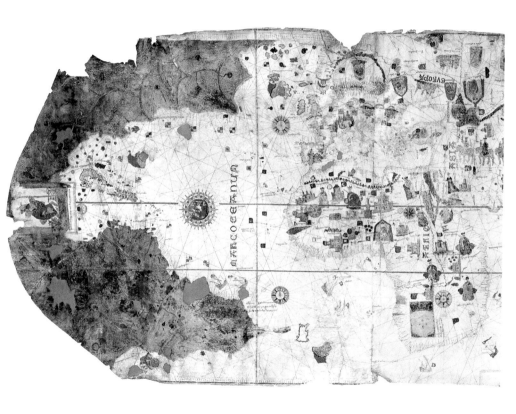

Discovering New Worlds, West and East: 1400-1500

Sailing Over the Edge

We wonder what anxieties and hopes went through the minds of those daring sailors who first intentionally ventured far out into the open sea. They had no knowledge of what heaven or hell was over the horizon: the superstitions and religions of their day contributed to both their fears and their confidences.

Greek Coasts

Unknown Artist, 1500 (?)
Parchment, 60 x 41 cm
Bibliothèque nationale de France, Paris

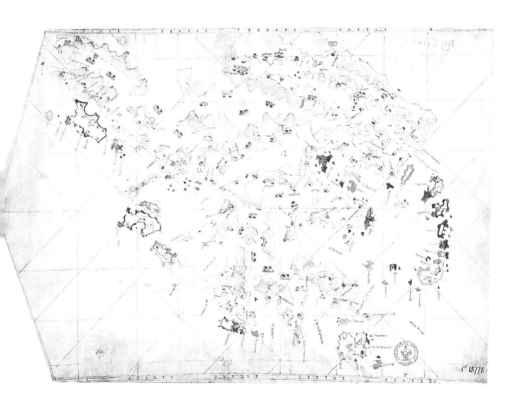

C.º 13778

Accordingly, the lands they discovered were given names of saints, and many of their ships also had names associated with religion. Many of those pioneers learned that it was wise to stay in sight of the coast, remembering and eventually recording memorable points. The tallest points and other notable landmarks were documented, named, and eventually became the sites of ports, giving rise in time to lists of ports and eventually charts and portolani.

Aegean Sea

Unknown Artist, 1500 (?)
Parchment, 73 x 40.4 cm
Bibliothèque nationale de France, Paris

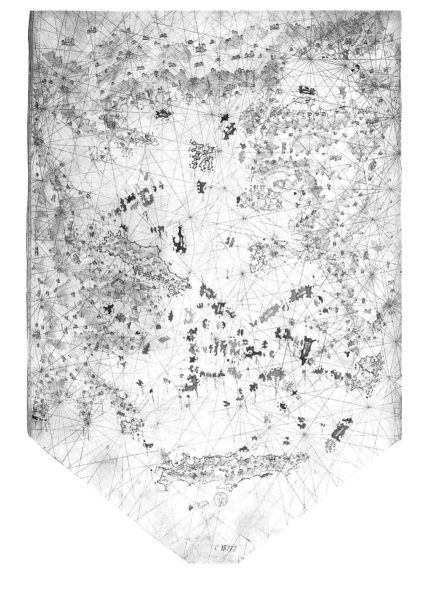

C 18777

John Cabot (c. 1450-1499)

When we think of the Age of Exploration, the names that first come to mind might will be those of the contemporaries Christopher Columbus and Vasco da Gama. However, more than a dozen years before the voyages of these pioneers, John Cabot envisioned and proposed reaching the Far East by sailing west. Soon, Cabot was among the first explorers from Europe after Columbus to reach the North American coast.

Just like Columbus before him, John Cabot returned to Europe with a wealth of new information to contribute to contemporary maps. We now know that much of Cabot's data was incorrect. Like Columbus, he too thought he had reached Asia.

Cantino's Planisphere

1502
Three parchment sheets, 220 x 105 cm
Biblioteca Estense, Modena

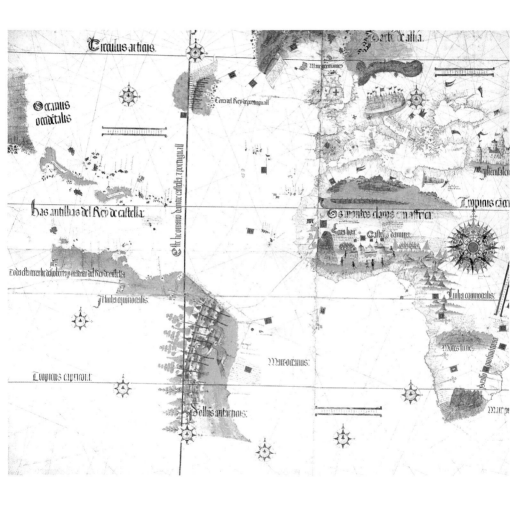

69

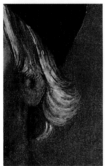

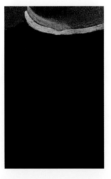

Christopher Columbus (c. 1451-1506)

As a young man Columbus was, among other things, a scholar and seller of maps. Seven years before his most famous voyage of 1492, he read and commented on a book in Latin that related the travels of Marco Polo. Like Fra Mauro, Columbus could hardly be aware of errors in Marco Polo's accounts. Similarly, Columbus had studied Ptolemy's maps. Columbus had no idea that Ptolemy had badly underestimated the circumference of the Earth. Columbus also studied Martin Behaim's globe (Map, p. 59) and Paolo Toscanelli's chart of the world, as described herein earlier.

Portrait of Christopher Columbus

Ridolfo Ghirlandaio (1483-1561), first half of the 16th century
Padiglione del Mare e della Navigazione, Gena

These authoritative resources were included in the presentation by Columbus first to the King of Portugal who rejected the proposal. He then tried for seven long years to make the same proposals to King Ferdinand and Queen Isabella of Spain. He finally got their backing and sailed the "ocean blue" in 1492.

Columbus returned to Spain with promises of endless conquests on behalf of the nation. Spain was on its way to building an empire in the Americas and eventually in the Philippines. Maps were vital, and required continual updating.

Planisphere
_____

Nicolaus de Caverio, c. 1505
Parchment, 115 x 225 cm
Bibliothèque nationale de France, Paris

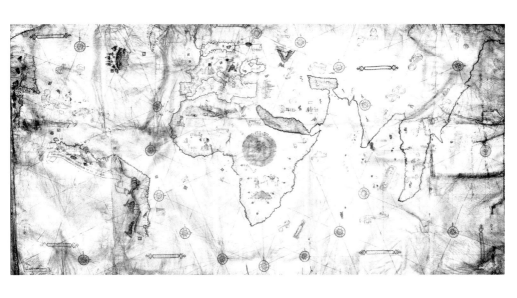

73

The de la Cosa map

In 1500, after four voyages Columbus, Juan de la Cosa of Santona drew his now famous map on oxhide (Map, p. 63). In the 19th century the map was discovered in Madrid by Alexander von Humboldt. It was the first of many maps to attempt to show all of Columbus' discoveries. His map takes on special significance since de la Cosa was on the Santa Maria with Columbus during the first voyage.

Portolan of Dijon

Unknown artist, c. 1510
Parchment (in irregular triangular format)
max. dimensions 99.5 x 66,5 cm
Bibliothèque municipale, Dijon

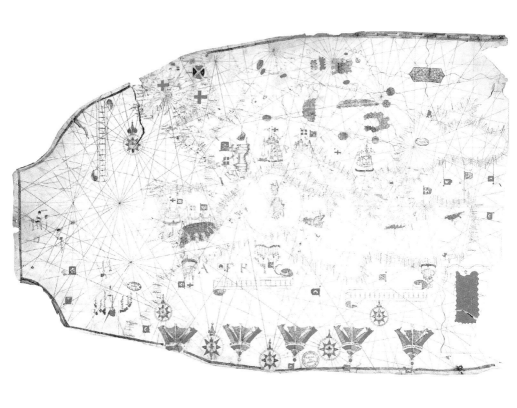

75

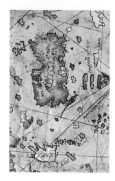

It shows the islands of the Caribbean curiously located between two continental coasts, and the coast to the west of the islands – where we might expect to find the most dramatic piece of new information – is actually obscured by a religious icon of St Christopher – not coincidentally the patron saint of Columbus.

The Three Pinzón Brothers
(Martin, c. 1441-1493 ; Vicente, c. 1460-c. 1523)
Together they have a unique page in the history of navigation. Francisco Martin and Vicente Yáñez not only became sailors, as had their older brother Martin Alonso before them,

Atlantic Ocean

Piri Re'is, 1513
Parchment, 90 x 65 cm
Topkapi Sarayi Museum, Istanbul

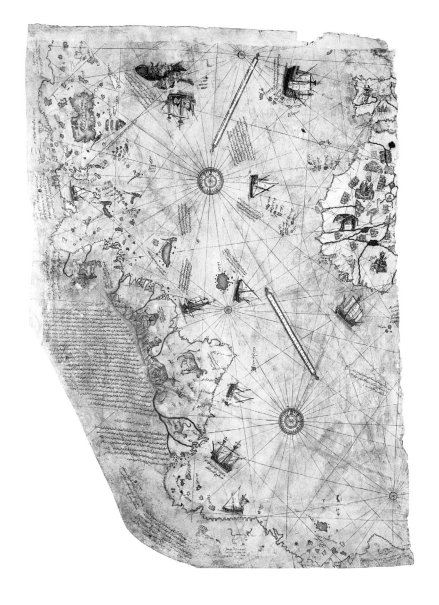

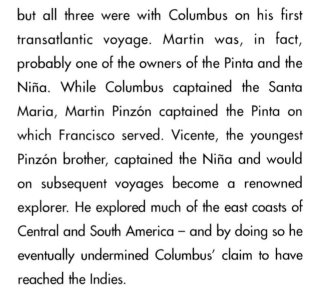

but all three were with Columbus on his first transatlantic voyage. Martin was, in fact, probably one of the owners of the Pinta and the Niña. While Columbus captained the Santa Maria, Martin Pinzón captained the Pinta on which Francisco served. Vicente, the youngest Pinzón brother, captained the Niña and would on subsequent voyages become a renowned explorer. He explored much of the east coasts of Central and South America – and by doing so he eventually undermined Columbus' claim to have reached the Indies.

The Miller Atlas (The Azores)

Lopo Homem and others, c. 1519
Parchment, 41.5 x 59 cm
Bibliothèque nationale de France, Paris

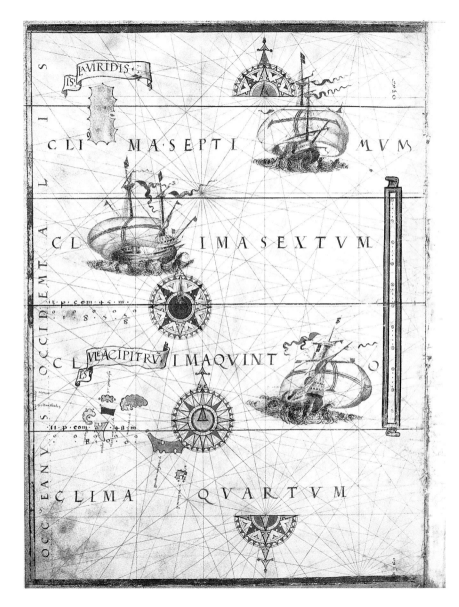

IS. LA VIRIDIS

CLIMA SEPTI MVM

CLIMA SEXTVM

LA ACIPITRV IS

CLIMA QVINT

CLIMA QVARTVM

OCCEANVS OCCIDEMTALIS

79

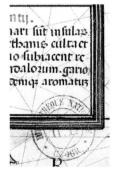

The cartographer Juan de Solfs accompanied Vicente on an expedition in 1506 during which a careful survey of the Yucatán Peninsula was made and an excellent natural harbor discovered in what is now Honduras. It would be settled and become the modern port of Trujillo. Meanwhile Juan de Solfs returned home, and subsequent portolani incorporated data from his detailed survey.

The Miller Atlas (Madagascar)

Lopo Homem and others, c. 1519
Parchment, 41.5 x 59 cm
Bibliothèque nationale de France, Paris

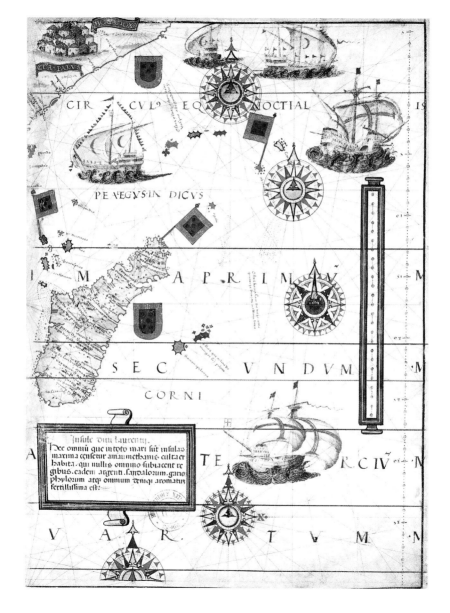

MOGADOXS

GOA PALYS

CIR CVL⁹ EQ NOCTIAL IS

PE⁹EGVS IN DICVS

I M A P R I M V M

S E C V N D V M M

CORNI

Infule dini Laurenty.
Dec omniu que in toto mari sut insulas
maxima cenfetur amaumethanus cultater
habita. qui nullis omnino fubiacent re
gibus. eadem argenti. fandalozum. gario
phylozum atq omnium ceniq aromatiz
fertilissima est:

A TE RCIV⁹ M

V A R. T V M M

Of the Pinzón brothers, it was to be Martín who would draw the most attention of historians, but not primarily because of his navigational skills. Rather, he is much better known for deserting Columbus for about six weeks once the expedition had reached Cuba. Seeking personal fortune, the impatient Martín ventured out on his own in search of an island described to him by the natives as being rich with gold. He never found that island – but he did discover Hispaniola before Columbus.

The Miller Atlas (Arabia and India)

Lopo Homem and others, c. 1519
Parchment, 41.5 x 59 cm
Bibliothèque nationale de France, Paris

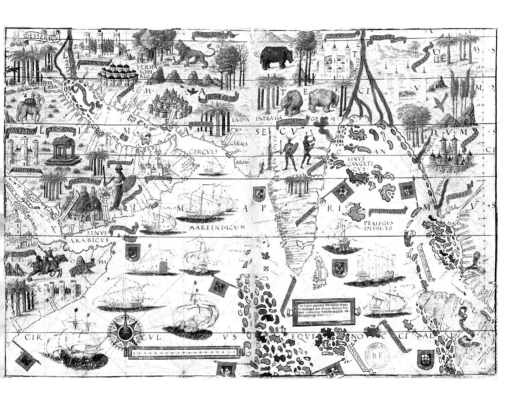

83

Juan Ponce de León (1460-1521)

Columbus' second expedition to the New World included a young crew member named Juan Ponce de León. After helping to suppress native revolts on Hispaniola, he was given his government's permission to take over the governorship of Puerto Rico. As further Spanish acknowledgement of his success, he was allowed to settle 'the island of Bimini'. A famous legend holds that Ponce de León was desperate to find the source of a rejuvenating tonic, the 'Fountain of Youth', described to him by Caribbean natives. Of course he never found anything of the sort – but he did discover Florida.

The Miller Atlas (Malaysia, Sumatra)

Lopo Homem and others, c. 1519
Parchment, 41.5 x 59 cm
Bibliothèque nationale de France, Paris

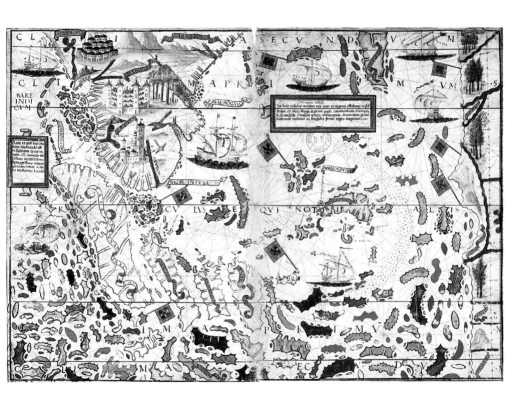

85

Amerigo Vespucci (1455-1512)

The reason for celebrity of the Italian explorer stems more in his first name than his actual journeys. Having explored the new world in 1499, he published the account of his travels in 1504 and dated his first exploration of 1497 before that of Christopher Columbus (1498), thus making himself appear to be the discoverer of the New World. Later in 1507, Martin Waldseemüller, a Saint-Dié geographer, published a work in which he named the new continent after its presumed discoverer. He must not have been aware of the accounts of Columbus, and thus made perpetual one of the biggest inaccuracies in history.

The Miller Atlas (Brazil)

───────────────────────

Lopo Homem and others, c. 1519
Parchment, 41.5 x 59 cm
Bibliothèque nationale de France, Paris

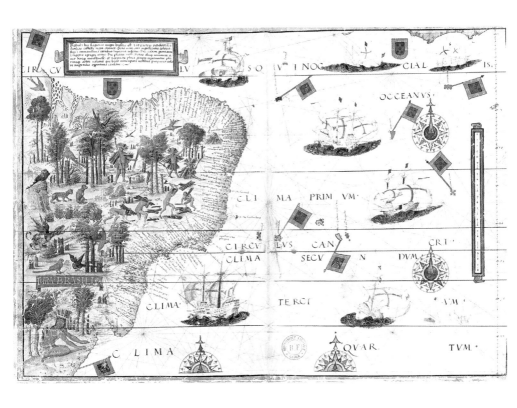

Bartolomeu Dias (?-1500)

Near the end of the 15th century gaining access to India's commerce was the most important goal for Portugal; that trade was vital to its commercial survival. It commissioned expeditions to India by sea as well as by land. In 1487, the Portuguese navigator, Bartolemeu Dias, was given a fleet of three ships and the assignment to find the southernmost point of Africa. Dias was also commanded to find Prester John, the mythical king of a large part of western Africa. He did not find the king, but in 1489, he did become the first European to successfully sail past the Cape of Good Hope.

The Miller Atlas (Atlantic)

Lopo Homem and others, c. 1519
Parchment, 61 x 118 cm
Bibliothèque nationale de France, Paris

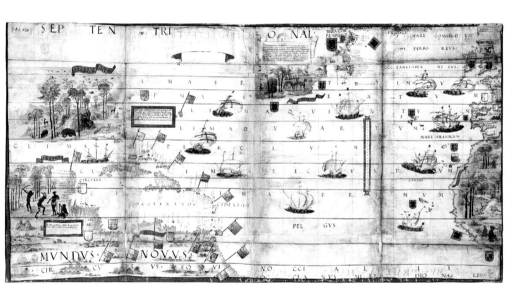

Vasco da Gama (1460-1524)

Vasco da Gama may have been only twenty nine when Columbus returned for the first time from the New World to Spain, but he was far from inexperienced. He had already learned navigation, mathematics, and astronomy and had also seen at first hand how to manage many people and large projects just like his father, the civil governor of Sines, in their home town in southern Portugal. His challenge was to find a route around Africa and across the Indian Ocean to India itself. He was put in charge of four vessels and 170 seamen. Unfortunately, Paolo would not be one of the fifty four survivors of the expedition.

Portrait of Vasco da Gama

Museum of Ancient Art, Lisbon

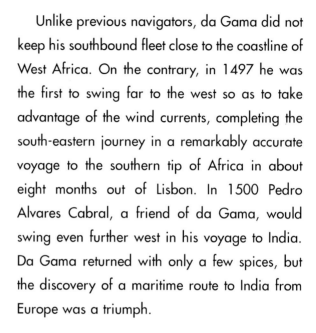

Unlike previous navigators, da Gama did not keep his southbound fleet close to the coastline of West Africa. On the contrary, in 1497 he was the first to swing far to the west so as to take advantage of the wind currents, completing the south-eastern journey in a remarkably accurate voyage to the southern tip of Africa in about eight months out of Lisbon. In 1500 Pedro Alvares Cabral, a friend of da Gama, would swing even further west in his voyage to India. Da Gama returned with only a few spices, but the discovery of a maritime route to India from Europe was a triumph.

Kitab-i-Bahriye ('The Book of the Seafarers') (Coast of Asia Minor)

Piri Re'is, 1525-1526
Parchment, 35 x 46 cm
Bibliothèque nationale de France, Paris

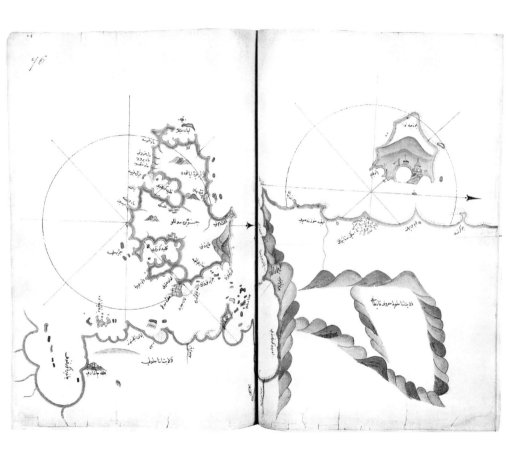

Portolani during this period

Portolani (such as Maps, p. 41, 43, 45, 47, 49, and 51) from the early part of the 15th century might well have been available to the older Pinzón, Cabot, Columbus, Vespucci and explorers after them. For del Canto, the younger Pinzón, Vasco da Gama, Ponce de León and subsequent navigators, many improved maps (such as in Maps, p. 53, 55 and 57) may have been available. The explorers active after the second half of the 15th century would have seen maps (p. 59 and 61) with even more detail. The famous maps of Columbus (Map, p. 61) and of Juan de la Cosa (Map, p. 63) are mentioned in the text above.

Kitab-i-Bahriye
('The Book of the Seafarers') (Crete)

Piri Re'is, 1525-1526
Parchment, 35 x 46 cm
Bibliothèque nationale de France, Paris

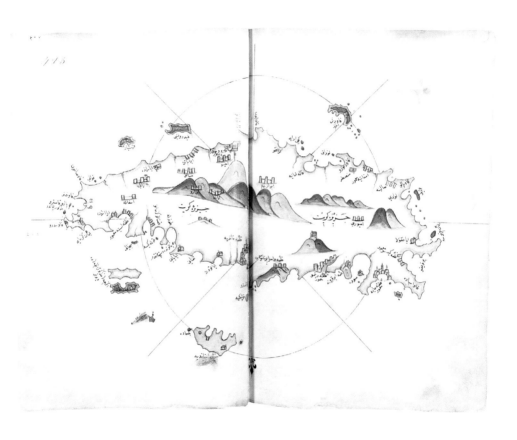

95

Independent Portolani

The Maps on p. 45 and 47, dated 1420, stand out from preceding schools. These maps were included in a best-selling book by Cristoforo Buondelmonte that was translated into Greek and Latin. The book with its maps introduced a new approach to marine cartography that was followed until the 17th century.

The Map on p. 51 is extremely rare, a real Catalan navigation map. While there is no interior nomenclature, descriptions of the Black and Mediterranean Seas are visible. Proportions within the whole basin are more exact than in previous maps.

World Map

Diogo Ribeiro, 1529
Parchment, 85 x 204.5 cm
Bibliotheca Apostolica Vaticana, Vatican

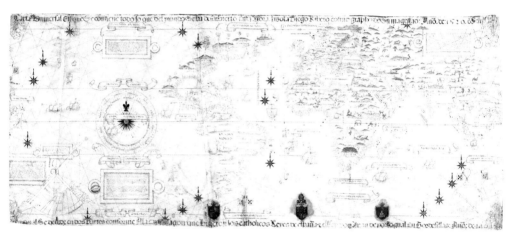

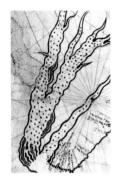

The Map on p. 53, a detail from a much larger map, has similar details and views of the most important cities. It also attempts to achieve the right proportions between the Atlantic and Mediterranean. Representation of the British Isles is greatly improved over that of previous maps, especially of the east coast and Ireland. The artist, Petrus Roselli, is one of the most important cartographers of the 15th century. This is one of only six known maps drawn up by him during his most productive period, 1447-1468.

The oldest known globe, made in 1492 under the direction of Martin Behaim, actually comprises pieces of parchment stuck onto a wooden sphere. The Map on p. 59 is a copy dating from 1847.

Atlantic Ocean

Gaspar Viegas, 1534
Parchment, 70 x 96 cm
Bibliothèque nationale de France, Paris

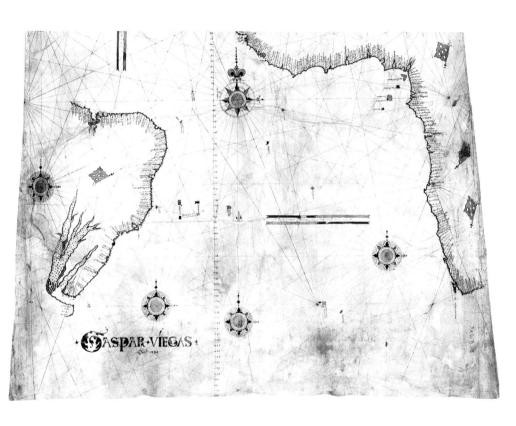

GASPAR·VIEGAS

The Dutch School

The Maps on p. 167, 189, 205 and 207 are of the Dutch school, centered in Amsterdam (1450-1548). They show the important influence of the English school at Bristol circa 1400. In turn they influenced the school at La Rochelle (1483-1559). The brothers Harmen and Marten Jansz made copies of maps, such as their very practical map of the Atlantic Ocean, the Mediterranean Sea and the Black Sea (Map, p. 167) of 1610. Colour-coded to help sailors distinguish territories, it is an example of the progress in Dutch cartography in the 16th century.

World Map
———————

Guillaume Brouscon, 1534
Parchment, 64 x 45 cm
Henry E. Huntington Library and Art Gallery,
Saint Marine

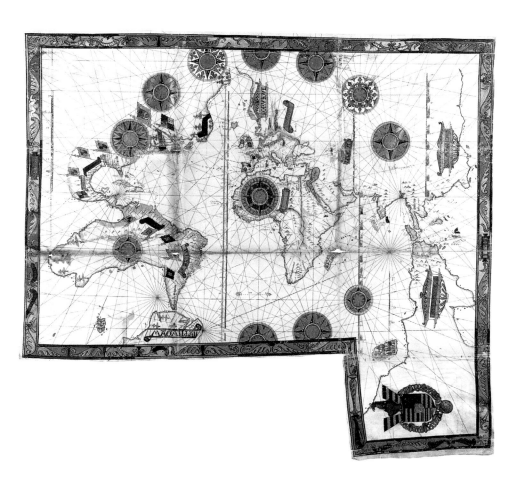

Beyond the New World: 1500-1550

Vasco de Balboa (c. 1475-1519)

The Spanish conquistador most identified with personal independence is undoubtedly Vasco Núñez de Balboa. After coming to the New World on a supply ship at about the age of twenty five, Balboa became a farmer but was soon in debt. In an effort both to escape his creditors and to avoid extradition to Spain, he smuggled himself aboard a ship bound from Hispaniola for Colombia.

The Boke of Idrography (Oriental India)

Jean Rotz, 1542
Paper, 59.5 x 77 cm
British Library, London

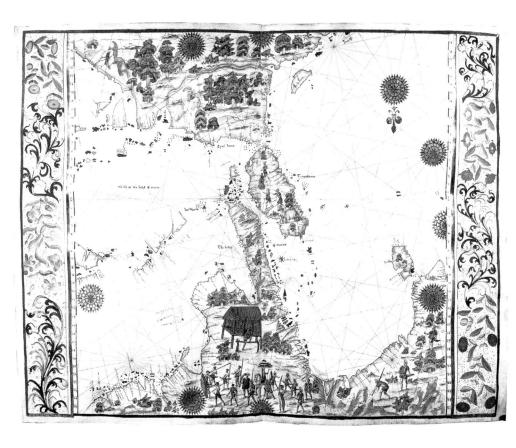

103

During a stopover in Cartagena, Balboa happened to meet Francisco Pizarro, who was to play an important role in the rest of his life. He went with Pizarro to Darién, the isthmus that we now know as Panama

In the Spanish colony in Darién, Balboa managed to take control from the governor appointed by King Ferdinand II of Aragon. As the self-appointed head of the village, he acquired native guides to help him travel west through the jungle.

The Boke of Idrography (Atlantic Ocean)

Jean Rotz, 1542
Paper, 59.5 x 77 cm
British Library, London

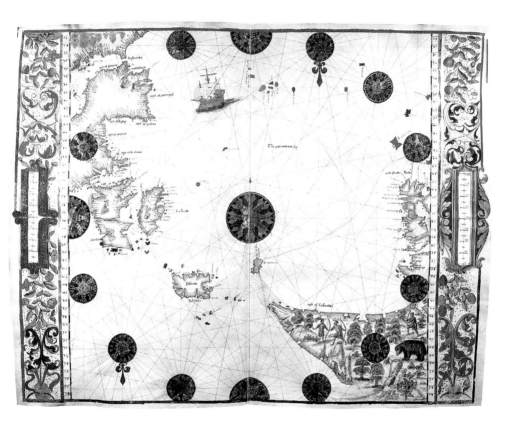

105

From a hilltop near the west coast on September 17, 1513, Balboa was the first European to see the Pacific from the Americas. Even though his expedition had been undertaken without the express approval of Spain, he carried the Spanish flag into the water and claimed not only the ocean for Spain but also all the islands surrounded by it.

Other Europeans, notably Marco Polo in the late 15th century, had reported seeing the ocean off Asia, but the idea in Europe that this was an ocean distinct from the Atlantic dates only back to Balboa's sighting. He named the ocean the Southern Sea.

World Map

Battista Agnese, 1543
Parchment, 19.5 x 29.5 cm
Bibliothèque nationale de France, Paris

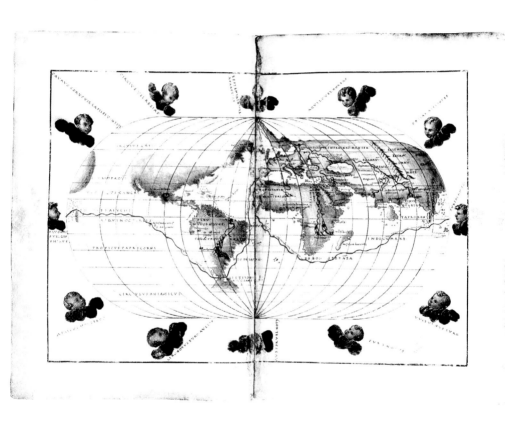

107

Ferdinand de Magellan (1480-1521)

Magellan was a page at the court of King Manuel I from the age of fifteen to twenty four. No doubt with the inspiring stories of the recent conquests of da Gama and Cabral fresh in mind, he joined an armada in 1504 that destroyed the fleets of Egypt and India, making Portugal at least as dominant as Spain as a power on the high seas. Perhaps because of accusations of illegal activity brought against him at court, Magellan renounced his Portuguese citizenship and convinced the young Spanish King, Charles, that he could reach the Southern Sea by sailing west.

Portrait of Fernand de Magellan

Municipal Museum, Sevilla

It would be the most ambitious exploration project ever. Spain was very interested in participating in the lucrative commerce with India and the Spice Islands. However, the 1494 Treaty of Tordesillas gave her rival, Portugal, access to those markets from the east, a possibility that was used successfully by da Gama and later by Cabral. To be able to reach the Spice Islands by sailing west would be like going through the back door of a house that they were forbidden to enter through the front door.

Pilot Manual for the use of Breton Mariners
(Atlantic maps)

––––––––––––

Guillaume Brouscon, 1548
Parchment, 27.5 x 31 cm
Bibliothèque nationale de France, Paris

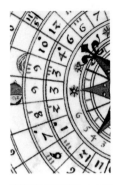

The First Voyage Around the World

The equipment Magellan took with him included twenty four portolani, or parchment maps, as well as a number of compasses, quadrants, astrolabes, hourglasses, and a copy of Faleiro's work on latitude. We know of such details thanks to one of the crew, Antonio Pigafetta, who in 1525 published a beautifully illuminated journal that has been used, along with the accounts of other survivors, to create a blow-by-blow account of the expedition.

Pilot Manual for the use of Breton Mariners
(Quadrante of the drizzles, Le Havre to Mores maps)

Guillaume Brouscon, 1548
Parchment, 17.5 x 14 cm
Bibliothèque nationale de France, Paris

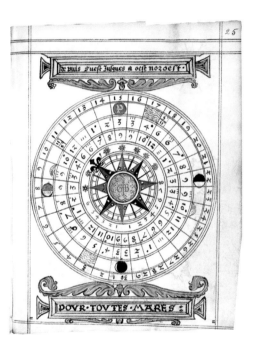

113

During his voyage southward along the South American coast, Magellan noticed the mouth of a channel, but of course had no way of knowing how far inland it went. He sent one of his ships into the channel to scout, but the crew was afraid to navigate further than the outlying strait. It was not unusual at that time for intelligent people still to believe in sea monsters. Having spotted penguins and other unfamiliar creatures for the first time, rumors of sea monsters spread through the superstitious sailors of the expedition. Instead of sailing west, the crew that was meant to be scouting ahead deserted and sailed their ship back to Spain.

Atlantic Ocean

Unknown Artist, after 1549 (c. 1550)
Parchment, 88 x 63 cm
Bibliothèque nationale de France, Paris

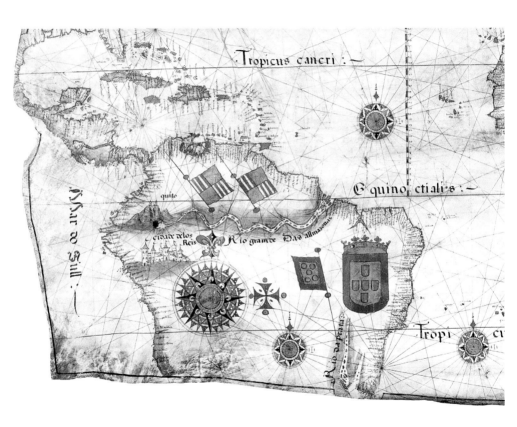

Tropicus cancri :—

Equino ctialis :—

Mar do Sull

quito

cidade delos Reis

Rio grande Das Allmasonas

Rio de prata

Tropi cu

115

It was up to Magellan himself then to carefully navigate the remaining ships through the difficult 350-mile waterway as they discovered what they had hoped for – a navigable passage to the Southern Sea. The passage would soon be called the Straits of Magellan. Meanwhile, Magellan called the ocean they reached 'Pacific', for its relative calm, compared to the turbulent waters through which he had just passed. During that historic 1521 voyage, Magellan pressed west across the ocean. Nobody knows exactly the route he took.

Atlantic Ocean

Diego Gutierrez, 1550
Parchment stuck onto paper, 131.8 x 88.5 cm
Bibliothèque nationale de France, Paris

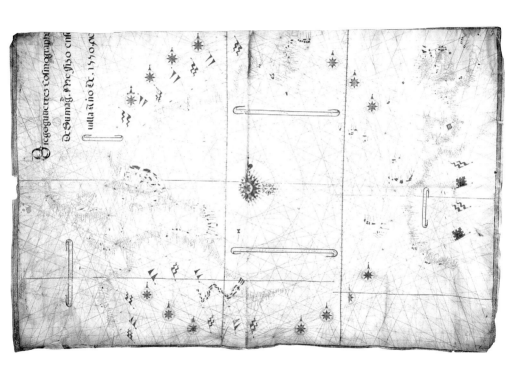

117

Jacques Cartier (1494-1554)

Cartier's original aim was, as it had been for a number of Europeans before him, to find the North West Passage to the Far East. In 1535, on the Feast of Saint Lawrence (August 10), Cartier reached a bay he named after the saint. With the help of local natives the mouth of the major river that flowed into the bay was found days later. Cartier called the river simply La Grande Rivière. The entire Gulf of St Lawrence and the St Lawrence River were given their names later by others. Cartier's voyage inland as far as present day Montreal was the foundation for France's later claim to Canada. The political landscape of North America would be thereafter influenced by the explorations of his small group of men.

World Map

Pierre Desceliers, 1550
Parchment, 135 x 215 cm
British Museum, London

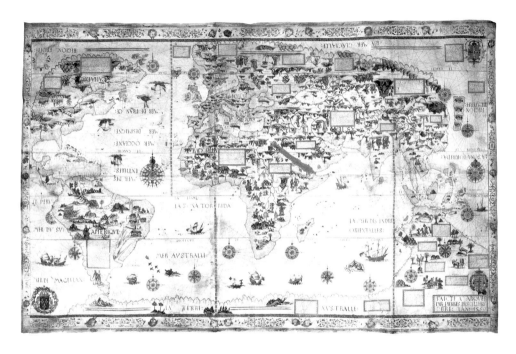

Portolani During This Period

Maps (like those on p. 63-69, 73-89, 93-107 and 111-113) available to Frobisher, Drake and Davis and their contemporaries in the 16th century could have been available, although of course it is unlikely that many of the pirate and privateer maps of the time were made public.

L'école portugaise
In this collection there are twenty three examples of the Portugese School at Lisbon (c. 1470-1706): Maps, p. 69, 75, 79-89, 115, 129-135, 143, 151, 177, 193-195, 201-203 and 221.

The World (Florida)

Guillaume Le Testu, 1556,
Paper, 37 x 53 cm
Service Historique de l'Armée de Terre, Vincennes

121

In the Map on p. 53 the nomenclature is in several Mediterranean languages. On each non-Muslim city between Ceuta and Venice, a banner identifies the city as Christian, reflecting the influence of the Crusades. The row of tents pictured in Africa are similar to those on the 1563 map by Giacomo de Maggiolo (Map p. 137). The Maps on p. 79-89 of the Miller Atlante are so named after their last owner. This atlas, considered a major work of art as well as significant source of maritime information, is unfortunately now incomplete. It once covered the entire known world before the Magellan discoveries. Portuguese banners on the maps show the important markets or new discoveries of that nation.

The World (The New France)

Guillaume Le Testu, 1556
Paper, 37 x 53 cm
Service Historique de l'Armée de Terre, Vincennes

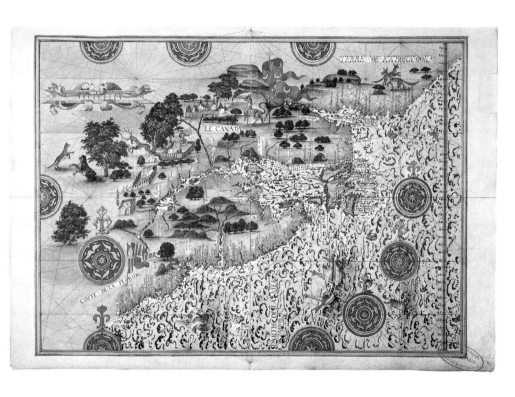

123

The miniatures of native birds, animals and fauna were done by Gregorio Lopes. The content shows the influence of Ptolemy's Geographia. Each map has a rhumbline system with sixteen secondary centers, a distance scale, and red lines to indicate the equator and the tropics.

Another Portuguese map of the Lisbon School is the anonymous map of the Atlantic made after 1549. In the Map on p. 115 exhibits the courts of arms and banners typical of major political landowners. The portolani of Diogo Homem (Maps, p. 129-133) and his brother Andreas Homem (Map, p. 135) would seem to reflect the influence of their father Lopo Homem, official cartographer to the King of Portugal.

The World (Terra Nova)

Guillaume Le Testu, 1556
Paper, 37 x 53 cm
Service Historique de l'Armée de Terre, Vincennes

125

Their works are dated 1559. The work of Andreas is the only one now known, whereas Diogo was possibly the most prolific Portuguese cartographer of his century, creating at least a dozen universal or Mediterranean atlases and eleven large maps. It would also seem, then, that the one brother created a large number of works, while the other may have been responsible for only one truly huge work. Andreas' ten parchment sheets comprise two rows of five sections making the resulting work the largest Portuguese nautical map of the Renaissance. His map displays a certain freedom from the limitations of Ptolemy's work.

The World (Java)
───────────────

Guillaume Le Testu, 1556
Paper, 37 x 53 cm
Service Historique de l'Armée de Terre, Vincennes

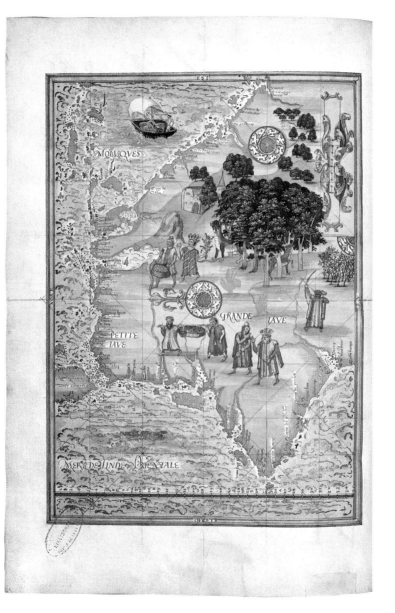

127

It shows the division of the known world markets into two parts according to the Treaty of Tordesillas: the Spanish to the west and the Portuguese to the east. The portolano of the Atlantic and the Mediterranean by Giacomo de Maggiolo (Map, p. 137) shows that he used a recent edition of Ptolemy's Geographia, at least when presenting Denmark and the Scandinavian Peninsula. But in this 1563 work there is also a new awareness of northern Europe. The Madonna and the infant Jesus are respectfully centered on the left side of the map.

Atlas (Occidental Europe)

Diogo Homem, 1559
Parchment, 44 x 58.6 cm
Bibliothèque nationale de France, Paris

The anonymous Portuguese universal map (Map, p. 151) attributed by the French to Pedro de Lemos was drawn up in around 1585. It includes, probably for the first time, the Philippine archipelago. Each hemisphere has its own rhumbline system. The influence of the Treaty of Tondesillas is seen on the map in the division of the world between the Spanish and the Portuguese. The 1618 Atlantic (Map, p. 177) is the only known map of Domingos Sanchez. Patron Saints are represented, especially St Joseph with the infant Jesus, also Saints Benedict, Leonard, Stephen and Barbara.

Atlas
(Oriental Atlantic and Occidental Mediterranean)

Diogo Homem, 1559
Parchment, 44 x 58.6 cm
Bibliothèque nationale de France, Paris

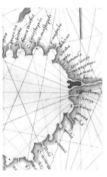

The Monomotapa Empire, south of the current Zimbabwe, was occupied by the Portuguese then by the Arabs from the 15th century to the 19th century. On the map of João Teixeira Albernas II (1677), the gold mines in the area are indicated. Portuguese merchants had their own security forces that regulated the circulation of gold and defied local authorities. The map maker became well-known following the publication of his 1665 atlas showing the African coasts. Years later, these maps were included in a work published in 1700 in Amsterdam.

Atlas (Black Sea)

———————

Diogo Homem, 1559
Parchment, 44 x 58.6 cm
Bibliothèque nationale de France, Paris

Rusia podolia SEPTENTRIO Tartaria ORIENS

Capestria

valachia Mengralia

Occidens.

Asia minor

Capadotia

TV
RQV
IA

Armenia.

133

The Spanish School
These portolani (Maps, p. 63 and 117) of the Spanish school at Seville (1508-1709) show the influence of 14th century Catalunia.

The Genovese and Viennese Schools
The important map of Juan de la Cosa (Map, p. 63) is discussed in some detail above. The map of the Atlantic by Diego Gutierrez of 1550 (Map, p. 117) employs a system of two gradations in latitude, but these were soon found to be impractical. In fact, Ferdinand Columbus, the son of Christopher, and Jean Rotz denounced these maps, saying they were merely confusing to seafarers.

Universa ac navigabilis totius
terrarum orbis descriptio

Etreas Homem, 1559
Parchment stuck onto paper, 150 x 294 cm
Bibliothèque nationale de France, Paris

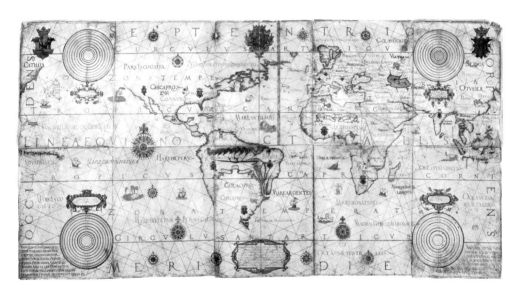

135

The Istanbul School

Portolani from the school centered in Istanbul (1513-1601) show the influence of the early examples of the Viennese school (Maps, p. 39, 41, 49, 55 and 57), while their style was not passed on to other major schools.

Piri Re'is, the author of the Turkish Map of the Atlantic (Map p. 95) in 1513, was born in 1470. His uncle had been a pirate but was later a multilingual commodore in the Ottoman navy at the end of the 15th century, who wrote an influential study of 16th century Mediterranean cartography.

Atlantic Ocean and Mediterranean Sea

Giacomo de Maggiolo, 1563
Parchment stuck onto parchment sheet, 102.3 x 85 cm
Bibliothèque nationale de France, Paris

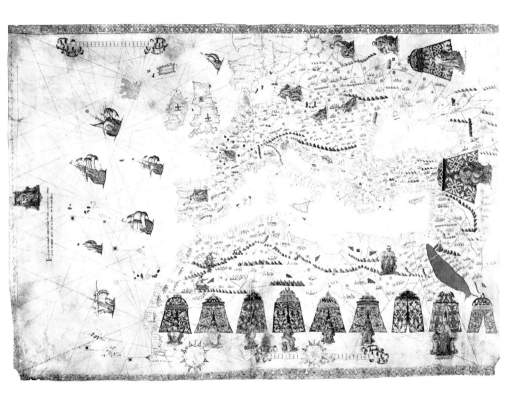

137

His nephew's map was discovered in 1929 during the reconstruction of the Topkapi Museum. The map shows only the eastern part of a larger and lost planisphere.

The two illuminated documents (Maps, p. 93 and 95) from a Turkish instruction book were also drawn up by Piri Re'is in about 1525-1526. The book comprised no fewer than 848 pages which included 215 nautical maps. Before its publication, many of the details it gives of the Mediterranean Sea had never been described.

The Mediterranean Basin

Giorgio Sideri (known as Calapoda), 1565
Parchment, 29 x 43 cm
Bibliothèque nationale de France, Paris

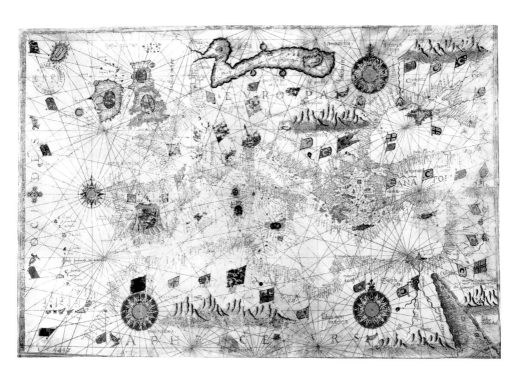

The Normandy School

In this presentation there are fourteen examples of portolani of the Normandy school centered at Dieppe (1536-1635): Maps on p. 103, 105, 119-127, 141, 147, 161, 171, 187, 191 and 199. These show the direct influence of the Portuguese School. The Normandy school in turn influenced the later English School in London (1579-1701) and subsequently the French School in Paris (1661-1751).

Pierre Desceliers' universal map (Map, p. 119) uses a 'walk-around' format. On the left appear the twelve climates of the Ptolemaic system from the equator to the poles.

World Map
———
Nicolas Desliens, 1566
Parchment, 27 x 45 cm
Bibliothèque nationale de France Paris

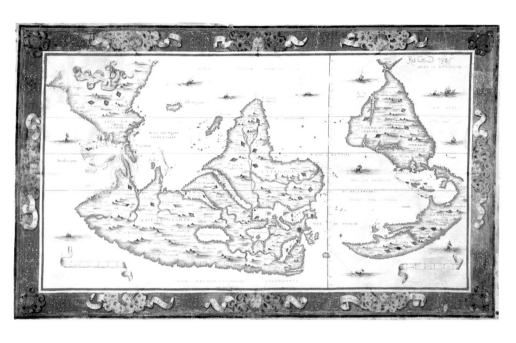

141

Four universal maps by Guillaume Le Testu (Maps, p. 121-127) from Normandy in the 16th century reflect the discoveries of Cartier. Scholars note that these maps perpetuate some of the errors of the Portuguese maps, but are an improvement over those of Rotz (Maps, p. 103 and 105).

The universal map of Nicolas Desliens (Map, p. 141) brings together all that was known at Dieppe at the time. This map, like many during the Renaissance, is oriented to the south (with north at the bottom of the map).

Atlas (Oriental India and Japan)

Fernão (Ferdinand) Vaz Dourado, 1571
Parchment, 54 x 40.5 cm
Instituto dos Arquivos Nacionais / Torre do Tombo, Lisbon

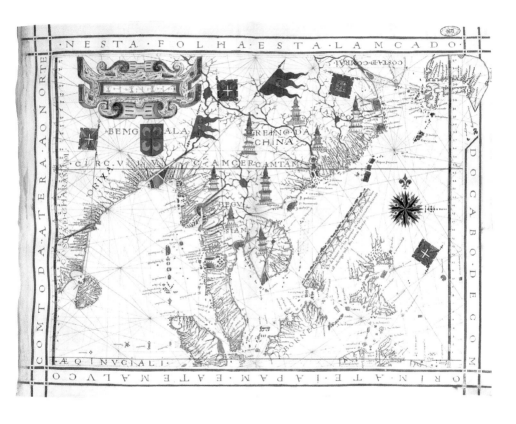

The only known portolani of Jacques de Vau de Claye are the two (Maps, p. 145 and 147) dated 1579. They show the Portuguese influence even though the nomenclature is in French. These are multi-purpose maps: nautical charts, in that coasts are detailed; economic maps, in that products (gold, amber, wood, sugar, cotton) are indicated; anthropological maps, in that the local Indian population is shown in their native dress; and natural history maps, in that rare birds and monkeys are illustrated.

Brazil

Jacques de Vau de Claye, 1579
Parchment, 59 x 45 cm
Bibliothèque nationale de France, Paris

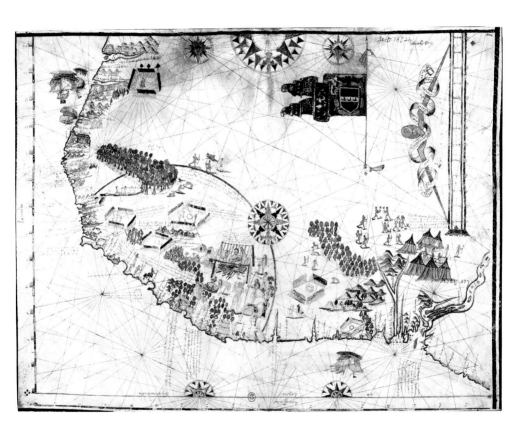

There is also a military purpose in showing the conquest of the Brazilian coast as imagined by Catherine de Medici (1519-1589), but her aim was never actually achieved because her troops were defeated in the Azores. There are many scholarly commentaries on this map.

The latitude crescent system instituted by Mercator in his 1569 world map influenced Guillaume Levasseur's Atlantic Ocean map of 1601 (Map, p. 161). Such maps were printed on parchment by the Dutch and distributed in Atlantic harbors. For the first time the name Quebec appears on a map of Canada. (Quebec was actually to be founded in 1608).

Rio de Janeiro Bay

Jacques de Vau de Claye, 1579
Parchment, 31 x 67 cm
Bibliothèque nationale de France, Paris

147

Along the St Lawrence River there are twenty eight other places with names that appear here for the first time. For identifying Canadian locations this may well be considered the most important map prior to Champlain's (Map, p. 165).

The portolani of the Atlantic Ocean by Pierre de Vaulx (Map, p. 171) include a French text and details about the new colonies in America, the ownership of each being indicated by courts of arms. There is no Portuguese banner. The coast of the Gulf of Mexico is described with more detail than on previous maps.

Atlas (South America)

Joan Martines, 1583
Parchment, 49.5 x 59 cm
Bibliothèque nationale de France, Paris

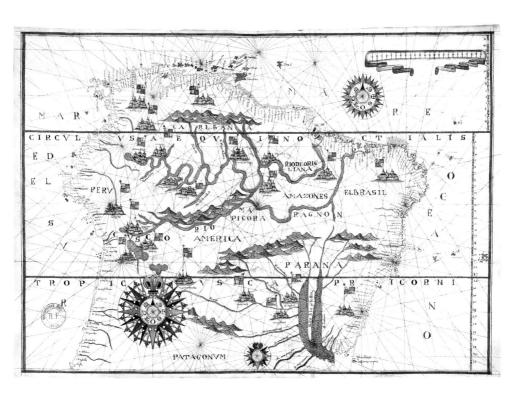

149

Bridging the Oceans: 1550-1600

Sir Francis Drake (c. 1540-1596)

Sir Francis Drake is acknowledged to be the most important British seaman and explorer of the Elizabethan age. Corsairs operated in the Mediterranean, specifically along the North African coast. Commanders, a crewmen, and even their armed ships could be called privateers if they had a commission from a bona fide government to capture merchant vessels of an enemy nation. As privateers sailed the coastlines seeking their enemy, they recorded valuable data for their own and future portolani to be used by future English seamen.

Portuguese Map of the World (Cyprus)

Unknown artist, c. 1585
Parchment, 114.5 x 218 cm
Bibliothèque nationale de France, Paris

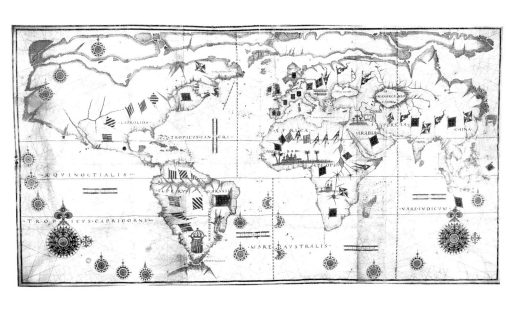

151

Drake also documented his voyage around the world. In 1577, at the outset of that historic three-year journey, Drake's crews were not aware of their ambitious goal to circumnavigate the globe. They were, therefore, astonished when they sailed past Gibraltar and the route to Egypt which they had believed to be their destination. Drake persevered, commanding his crew to sail across the Atlantic to Brazil, and by so doing became the first Englishman to sail through the Straits of Magellan. After passing through the strait, and instead of sailing directly north-east to the Philippines as Magellan had done about sixty years earlier, Drake sailed northward along the Pacific coast.

Atlas (Cyprus Isle)

Joan Martines, 1587
Parchment, 58 x 80 cm
Biblioteca Nacional de España, Madrid

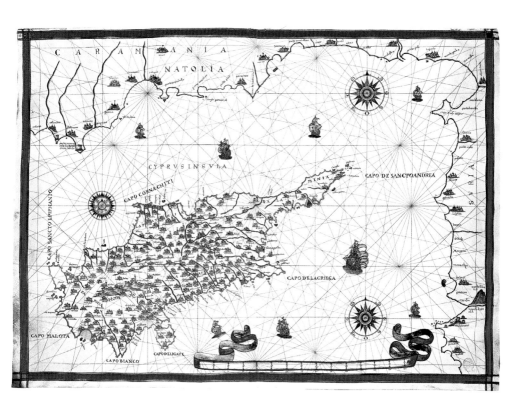

153

He then sailed for two months across the Pacific before landing in the Philippines, where he bartered with friendly natives, some acting as navigational guides through the archipelago. He documented his sightings and provided very valuable information for future Europeans to visit the area. He sailed west across the Indian Ocean, swung in a wide loop around the southernmost point of Africa (Cape Agulhas) and turned north to return to Plymouth. There, he was immediately greeted as a national hero. A few months after his return to Plymouth, Drake was knighted. He died at sea in 1596.

Atlas (South East Asia)

Joan Martines, 1587
Parchment, 58 x 80 cm
Biblioteca Nacional de España, Madrid

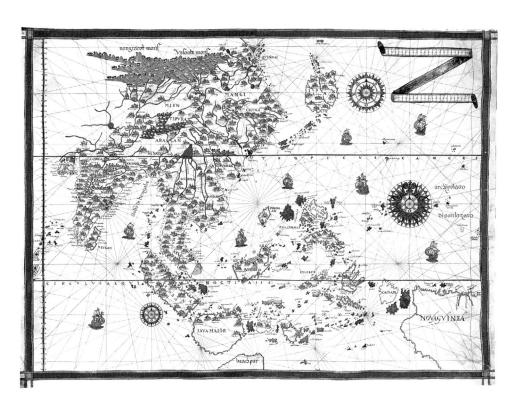

155

Jean François de La Pérouse (1741-1788)

During the first decade of American independence, the future 49th state of the United States was visited in 1786 by a French expedition – an expedition approved by Louis XVI and commanded by Jean François de La Pérouse, appointed captain four years earlier at the age of forty. He reached the west coast of Alaska. Portolani of the coastlines between Monterey and Alaska were developed in an effort to continue the work of Cook as the French made further claims to north-western territories. The French did not establish sovereignty in this region. However, La Pérouse was one of the discoverers of the eastern coast of New Caledonia. He and his two ships were lost in a Pacific storm in 1789.

Map of the Port-des-Français

1797
in L'Atlas du voyage de la Pérouse
Private Collection

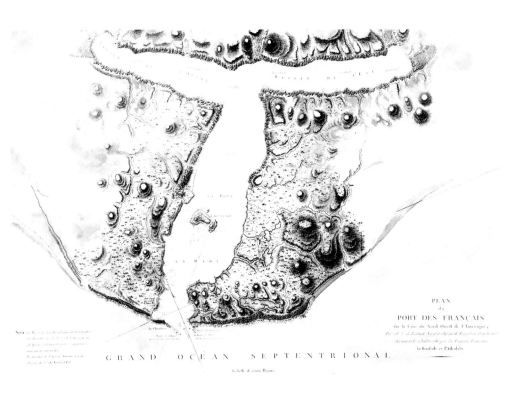

PLAN
du
PORT DES FRANÇAIS
sur la Côte du Nord-Ouest de l'Amérique,

GRAND OCÉAN SEPTENTRIONAL

Samuel de Champlain (c. 1567-c. 1635)

If there was one founder of New France or the future Canada, it was the French explorer Samuel de Champlain. In 1605, along with Pierre du Guast, Lord de Monts (1560-1611), he founded the first European settlement, later to become Montreal. Before founding Quebec, Champlain led pioneering trips up the St Lawrence and other rivers, reaching Lake Huron and Lake Ontario and finally discovered the lake that bears his name. At that particular time he was accompanied by a war party of the Algonquins and Hurons, actively supporting their eventual victory over the Iroquois near the present Ticonderoga.

Mediterranean Sea
_____

Nicolaos Vourdopolos, c. 1600-1610
Parchment, 50.5 x 59 cm
Bibliothèque nationale de France, Paris

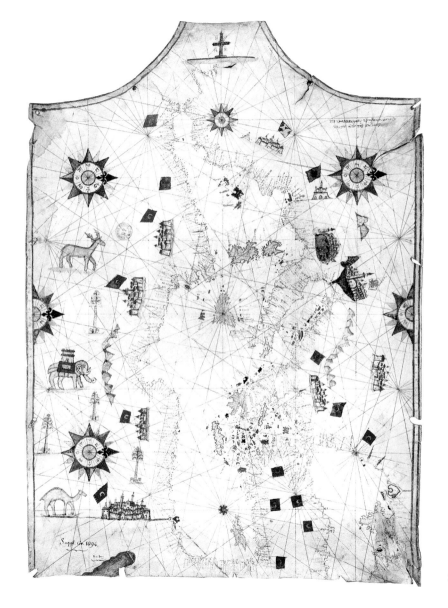

Before returning to France he commissioned others to carry on, including Jean Nicolet (who crossed Lake Huron and Lake Wisconsin) and Etienne Brulé, who sailed the Susquehanna River down to Chesapeake Bay. Today it is difficult to appreciate the fact that these 17th century explorers were envisioning a link through these rivers of New France to China. While it may seem comical to us nearly 400 years later, Peter Whitfield reminds us of the story of Nicolet, who so expected to be greeted by people of Asia, that he 'donned Chinese robes when he landed on the western shore of Lake Michigan.'

Atlantic Ocean

Guillaume Levasseur, 1601
Parchment, 74.4 x 99 cm
Bibliothèque nationale de France, Paris

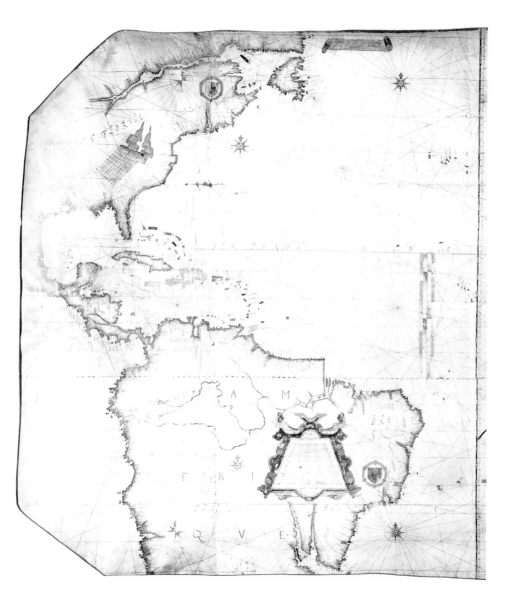

Portolani During This Period

The Breton School
Examples of portolani of the Breton school (1543-1650) centered at Le Conquet, inlcude Maps on p. 101, 111 and 113. These show the influence of the Portugese School at Lisbon.

A pilot's practical and simple pocket guide filled with useful charts and maps was made in 1548 by Guillaume Brouscon (Maps, p. 111 and 113). It tells amateur sailors how to take basic astronomical measurements for navigation, and includes a perpetual calendar and drawings of boats. A large map was folded into the volume.

Atlantic Ocean,
Mediterranean Sea and Black Sea

———————————————

Francesco Oliva, 1603
Parchment, 54 x 90 cm
Bibliothèque nationale de France, Paris

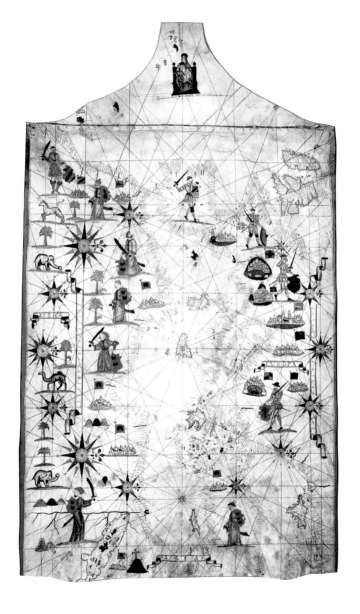

163

It presents the Atlantic coasts and the islands of the Baltic Sea, and the flags of eleven different nations, a French dictionary and the scale for calculating latitude. Several different editions of this guide exist, for it was a significant contribution to the navigation of the North Atlantic and adjacent oceans.

The Later Genovese School

Map 56 is of the Genovese School (up till 1588). Like the earlier works in this school, it was influenced by The Pisana (Map, p. 15) of the 13th century. Works of this school influenced the Viennese, Portugese, Spanish and Italian schools.

Description of New France

Samuel de Champlain, 1607
Parchment, 37 x 54.5 cm
The Library of Congress, Washington, D.C.

165

The Map on p. 165, the first cartographic work of de Champlain – the portolano of 1607 – shows the direct influence of the Dutch and Portugese schools. It influenced the Spanish and Breton schools. It is a description primarily of the coasts of New France and New England. To fully appreciate the work it should be studied along with his book Les Voyages du Sieur de Champlain, Saintongeois (1603), and his diary documenting his journey in Arcadia from 1604 to 1607. His map represents a new approach to geographical documentation based only on first hand observation.

North Eastern Atlantic Ocean,
Mediterranean Sea and Eastern Black Sea

Harmen and Marten Jansz, c. 1610
Parchment, 85 x 71 cm
Bibliothèque nationale de France, Paris

NOVA
ZEMLA

YSLANT

Noorwe
GEN

SWEDEN

oostvinlandt

RUSSIA

LVFLANDT

COURLANT

EUROPA

Pomerin PRVYSSEN

Hongaria

FRANCIA.

Province

SLAVONIA

Moldavia

Bulgaria

GRÆCIA

Garcenne

HISPANIA
Collia
CASTILIA.

NATOLIA

BARBARIA.

MAROC
CUS

MARMARICA
BARCHA

ÆGYPTVS

167

The Greek school

Maps on p. 139 and 159, of the Greek School (1537-1620), centered on Crete, show the influence of the 15ᵗʰ century Venetian school but are thought probably not to have influenced subsequent schools.

The Renaissance of Discovery: 1600-1700

Henry Hudson (c. 1550-1611)

Englishman Henry Hudson's voyage of 1610-11 continued the search for a North West Passage to the Pacific Ocean that fellow countryman John Davis had endeavored to find over twenty years before Davis went the furthest north into the strait

The Last Voyage of Henry Hudson

John Collier (1850-1934), 1881
Oil on canvas, 214 x 183.5 cm
Tate Gallery, London

now named for him, whereas Hudson went the furthest west, into the vast bay he soon realized was not the Pacific. His fourth voyage traveled beyond Davis's own exploration up Davis' Strait.

Both English and Dutch claims to North American lands were advanced by the explorations of Hudson. An English company paid for his first voyage, but his second was for the Dutch East India Company. Dutch claims on the territory would include the area that became New Amsterdam, and then New York City. It began with Hudson's second voyage when he sailed up the river that would eventually be named for him to the area of present day Albany.

Atlantic Ocean

Pierre de Vaulx, 1613
Parchment, 68.1 x 95.8 cm
Bibliothèque nationale de France, Paris

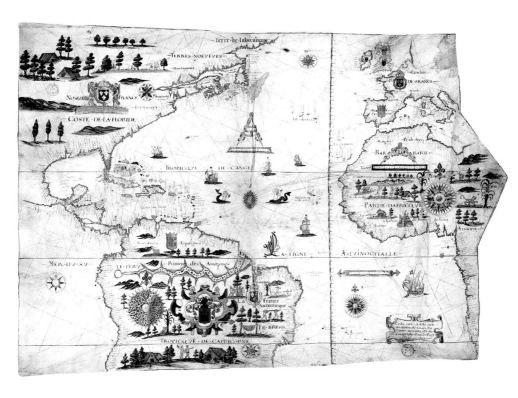

171

The portolano that Hudson used actually already indicated the strait, bay, and river, but he would probe and document them more extensively than any of the European explorers who preceded him.

Abel Janszoon Tasman (c. 1603-c. 1659)
The greatest of Dutch navigators, Abel Janszoon Tasman, is most obviously associated with the discovery of the island now named Tasmania. However, Tasman is less recognized for his other achievements that are just as great: the discovery of New Zealand, and Tonga, and the Islands of Fiji.

Portrait of Abel Tasman,
his Wife and Daughter
_____

Jacob Gerritsz Cuyp (1594-c.1651)
Oil on canvas, 106.7 x 132.1 cm
National Library of Australia, Camberra

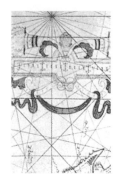

Tasman was also the first European to circumnavigate Australia. Several of his countrymen had already explored portions of the north and west coasts of 'the Southern Land' (Terra Australis), but Tasman proved that it was a vast continental island. In doing so, he also took soundings to document the water's depth around the entire coast of Australia. Tasman's contribution to mapping is momentous. He was the first to map the coastline of the Gulf of Carpentaria, which he also probably named.

Map of Japan from the Indian Ocean

Unknown Artist, c. 1613
Parchment, 96.5 x 63 cm
National Museum, Tokyo

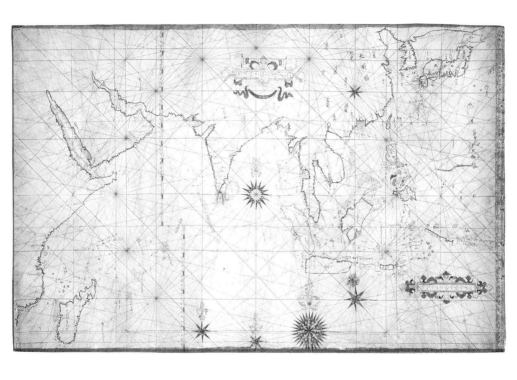

Portolani During This Period

The early 17th century explorers of the New World including de Champlain, Hudson, and Baffin, and the explorers of the Pacific including Tasman, created and had available to them maps (similar to Maps on p. 113-155) that were beginning to look like our own present day ones. Explorers of the 17th century including Marquette and Dampier could have known of maps (such as Maps on p. 159-171, 175-211, 215-217 and 221) that included a considerable quantity of authenticated data, reflecting the centuries of navigation prior to them.

Atlantic Ocean

Domingos Sanchez, 1618
Parchment, 95 x 84 cm
Bibliothèque nationale de France, Paris

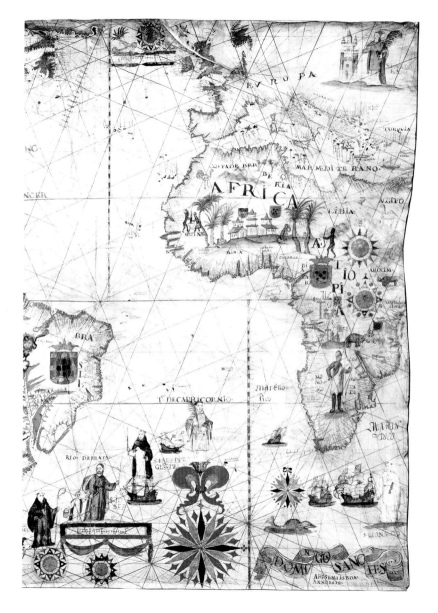

177

The Marseille School

Maps on p. 179, 197 and 209 are of the Marseille School (1590-1672). They show the marked influence of the school at Messina (1537-1620) and in turn they influenced the Paris School (1661-1751).

Five parchment sheets were used in 1620 by Charlat Ambrosin for his map of the Mediterranean (Map, p. 179). It introduced inset maps-within-the-map, showing three details, each with a different compass orientation: Malta (in the lower right), Sicily and the North African coast. Interiors, such as that of Tunis, are exceptionally detailed for the time.

Atlas of the Mediterranean

Charlat Ambrosin, 1620
Parchment, 47 x 67 cm
Bibliothèque nationale de France, Paris

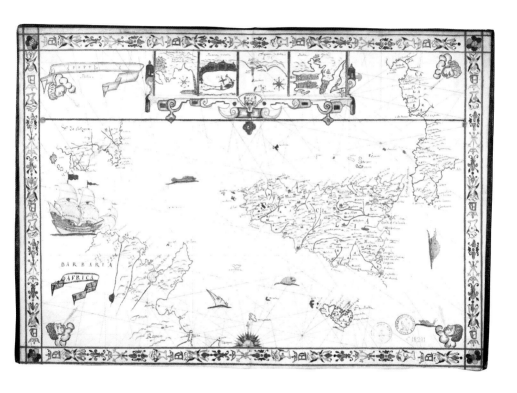

Creefts Sonnewend of Hooder Soun

Pry Hollel Gerreits.
anet Overray
vande E. H. M. Heeren
de Staten Generael,
der Vereenichde Nederlanden,
ift, bevonden.

i. dat is Steenhoex Sonnewend of

The Japanese School

The portolani of the Japanese School centered in Nagasaki (1592-1636) show the influence of only the Portuguese School. See, for example, the anonymous maps of Japan viewed from the Indian Ocean (Map, p. 175), or from the archipelago (Map, p. 185). The first Portuguese journey to Japan was in 1541-1543. It was the beginning of an important commercial relationship between the two countries. During the next forty-seven years (1543-1590) eighty ships arrived in Japan from Portugal.

The Pacific Ocean

Hessel Gerritsz, 1622
Parchment, 107 x 141 cm
Bibliothèque nationale de France, Paris

The Viennese School

The Map on p. 183 is of the Viennese School (1367-1690). Along with earlier examples from this school (Maps, p. 39, 41, 49, 55, 57) it shows the influence of the Genovese School. Earlier examples influenced the Spanish and Turkish Schools.

The Basque School

The Maps on p. 215 and 227 of the Basque School (1579-1690), centered at Saint Jean de Luz, show the influence of the 15th century school at La Rochelle (1493-1559). The map of the North Atlantic (Map, p. 215) by Denis de Rotis in 1674 reflects Basque-French commercial activity during the 17th century.

Aegean Sea

Alvise Gramolin, 1624
Parchment, 107 x 65 cm
Bibliothèque nationale de France, Paris

183

They had 39 whaling ships and 20 trawlers, monopolizing the whaling industry until the end of the 18th century. Note Labrador at the top of the map and the 'North West Passage' (Hudson's Bay) clearly indicated north of Canada. The other map of the Basque school (Map, p. 227), drawn up fifteen years after the de Rotis map, represents the coasts frequented most by the Basques.

The Late English School
English School Maps on p. 211, 217, 223, 229, 231 and 233 of the late 16th century show the influence of the Spanish (1508-1709) and Normandy (1536-1635) Schools.

The Japanese Archipelago

Unknown Artist, 1625
Parchment, 91.5 x 69 cm
National Museum, Tokyo

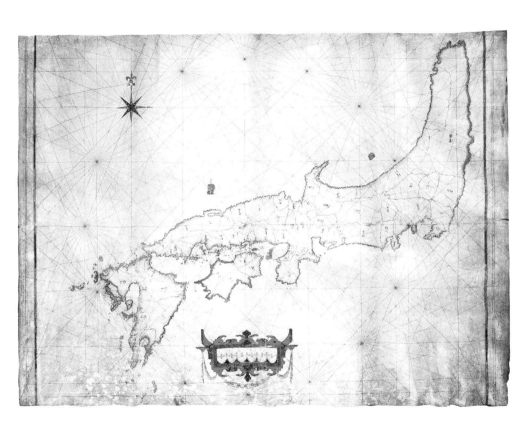

185

An anonymous portolano (Map, p. 217) dated 1675 reflects the recent explorations of Frobisher, Davis, Hudson, Button, and Baffin. However, there are many geographical mistakes in it, such as the absence of the Frobisher coast and the incorrect orientation of Labrador. Again, as elsewhere (Map, p. 215), Hudson's Bay is called 'the North West Passage'. The small port of Mocha (in what is now Yemen) became an important commercial center for the coffee trade during the 17th century.

The portolano by Augustine Fitzhugh (Map, p. 223) dated 1683 was made one year after the English market was established. There are two views: one on a bright day and the other on a cloudy day.

Nautical Guide to France
(Description hydrographique de la France)

Jean Guérard, 1628
Parchment stuck onto one parchment sheet, 120.5 x 81 cm
Bibliothèque nationale de France, Paris

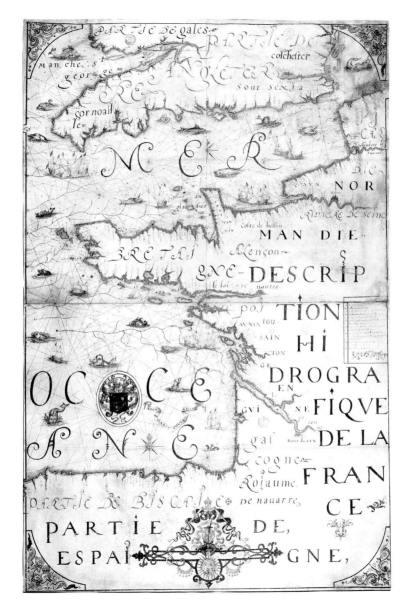

187

A long text gives navigation instructions and precautions. The cartographer describes the place and access to it as if he had been on an expedition there himself. Nutmeg and other spices come from a group of Indonesian islands called the Banda Isles (Map, p. 229) that resulted from volcanic eruptions centuries ago. The large anonymous map indicates the routes and distances between the three principal islands of Banda, Naira and Gunape. Discovered by the Portuguese, they were controlled by the Dutch in the 17th century. The last two portolani in the collection are beautiful examples of the Thames School by John Thornton, an apprentice between 1656 and 1664 of John Burston (Map, p. 211).

North Atlantic Ocean

Hessel Gerritsz, c. 1628
Parchment, 112 x 87 cm
Bibliothèque nationale de France, Paris

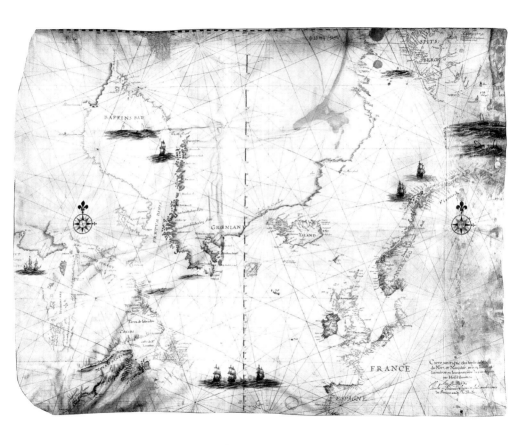

189

He was the cartographer for the maps for all of the voyages of the Hudson's Bay Company and the East India Company. He produced forty four manuscripts between 1667 and 1701, but he was famous for his atlas called The English Pilot that included thirty five maritime maps published for the first time in London in 1683. The map of the Persian/Arabian Gulf (Map, p. 231) is in Dutch and includes the discoveries of Cornelius Cornelisz Roobker in 1645. His map of Amoy Bay (Map, p. 233) is based on original observations made by the English during voyages along the Chinese coasts.

The Northern Ocean

Jean Guérard, 1628
Parchment stuck onto one parchment sheet, 86 x 128 cm
Bibliothèque nationale de France, Paris

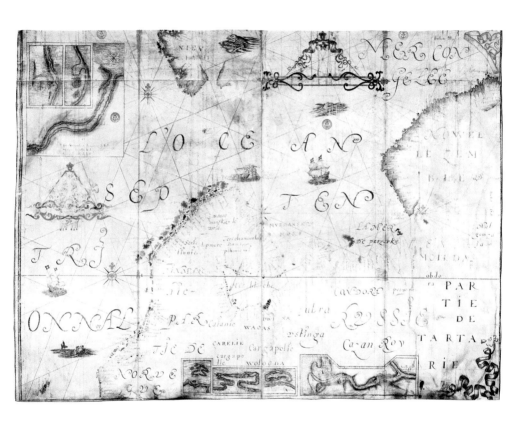

191

The French School

The French School portolano (Map, p. 213), circa 1660, benefited from being influenced by the 16th century schools at Amsterdam, Dieppe, London, and Marseilles. The map, dated 1666, is from the time of historic economic reconstruction in France, at the time when Jean Baptiste Colbert (1619-1683) was the finance minister to Louis XIV (from 1658 until his death). From 1668 to 1672 Colbert was particularly concerned with building up the French navy.

Atlas

———

Unknown Artist, c. 1630
Parchment 27 x 38 cm
Bibliothèque nationale de France, Paris

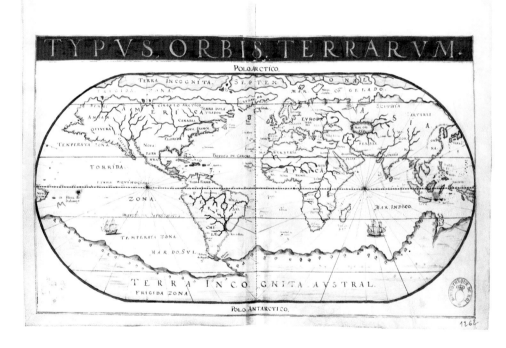

TYPVS. ORBIS. TERRARVM.

POLO ARCTICO.

TERRA INCOGNITA. SEPTEN TRIONAL

MAR CO GELADO.

FRIGIDA ZONA

SCITHIA

AMERICA

TARTARIA

ANIAN

CIRCVLO ARCTICO

TERRA INOLA VISADOS

ASIA

QVIVIRA

CANABA

EVROPA

NOVA FRANCA

NOVA

FLORIDA

TEMPERATA ZONA

TROPICO DE CANCRO

TORRIDA

TIERRA EQVINOCIAL

TERRA FIRME

AFRICA

MAR INDICO

ZONA

TROPICO CAPRICORNIO

CHI LE

TEMPERATA ZONA

MAR DO SVL

TERRA INCO GNITA AVSTRAL.

FRIGIDA ZONA

POLO ANTARCTICO.

Sailing Towards the Modern World: 1700-1900

James Cook (1728-1779)

In the portolani drawn up before the time of Magellan, we see that European map-makers imagined that the South Pacific was much smaller than in fact it is. Instead the cartographers envisioned a large land mass occupying most of the area. They named it Terra Australis Incognita (the Unknown Southern Land). The great English navigator James Cook would finally destroy this myth.

Atlas (Peru Coasts)

———————

Unknown Artist, c. 1630
Parchment, 27 x 38 cm
Bibliothèque nationale de France, Paris

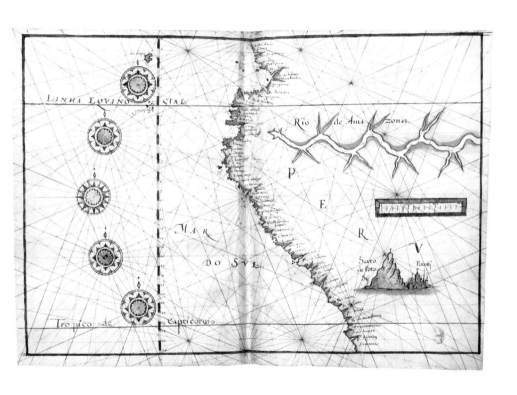

LINHA EQVINOCIAL

Rio de Ama zonas.

P

MAR

E

R

DO SVL

V

Cerro
de Poto
Sij

Potossi

Tropico de Capricornio.

195

Several explorers before Cook had shown the envisioned continent to be smaller by virtue of sailing through areas anticipated by these earlier maps to be part of this land. Cook himself did this first on his way to Tahiti in 1769. He was unique for his day in his more realistic estimate of the size of Antarctica, the actual southern continent.

James Cook was born in 1728 – the year Vitus Bering discovered the important passage that was named the Bering Strait after him. Fifty years later, Cook would also be drawn to that location. One of the assignments Cook was to carry out during his first voyage around the world was to observe

Provençal Atlas of the Mediterranean

Augustin Roussin, 1633
Parchment, 27.7 x 39.4 cm

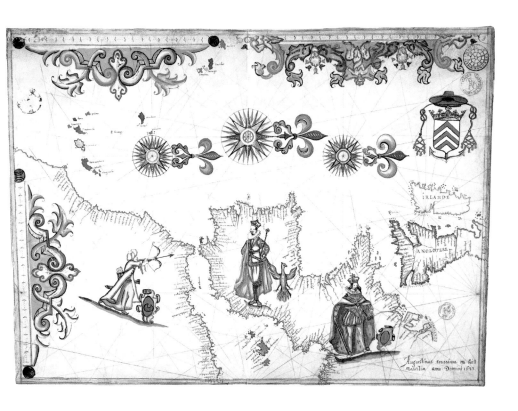

197

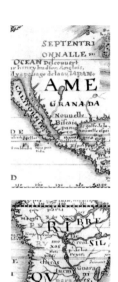

an exceptional astrological event: the 1769 transit of the planet Venus. The transit was an event of global importance, for astronomers around the world were hoping to gather data. Cook's first voyage was to achieve several important goals besides documenting the life he found in these strange new lands.

The year 1642 was pivotal for science: Galileo Galilei died, Isaac Newton was born, and Abel Tasman reached New Zealand, albeit believing that he was seeing the coast of the fabled Great Southern Continent, with a bay interrupting the coast. The next European to explore the same location was Cook, over a century later.

Nautical World Map
_____

Jean Guérard, 1634
Parchment, 39.6 x 47.9 cm
Bibliothèque nationale de France, Paris

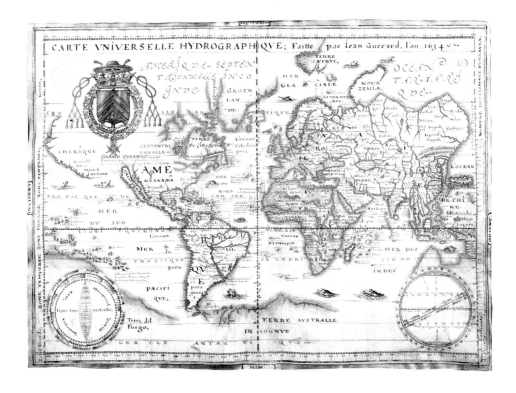

He found that what his predecessor had thought was a continent's coastline with a bay was in fact two islands divided by a strait – now Cook's Strait. The islands would later be named New Zealand.

His assignments completed, Cook could return to England. But instead he sailed to New Holland, later to be named Australia. He knew of Tasman's discovery of a century earlier, but map makers still did not know if Tasmania was an island or a peninsula of Australia. Unfortunately, bad weather kept him from finding out. The question remained unanswered for at least twenty years more.

Indian Ocean

João Teixeira Albernas, 1649
Parchment, 84.5 x 70.5 cm
Bibliothèque nationale de France, Paris

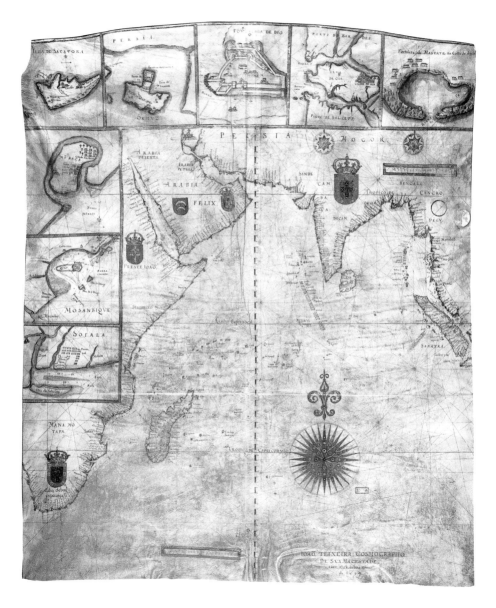

Cook went on to be the first European in over a century to pass through the Torres Strait, confirming it as a passageway between Australia and New Guinea. On the plus side, after Cook's first voyage New Zealand and Australia were now known to be islands and might be added to the British Empire. However, it was still not proved that the Great Southern Continent existed. So a second around-the-world voyage was commissioned, with hopes that the southern latitudes would be fully explored. In 1772, on Cook's second voyage, the men in his fleet were the first on record to cross the Antarctic Circle.

Pacific Ocean

João Teixeira Albernas, 1649
Parchment, 89 x 74 cm
Bibliothèque nationale de France, Paris

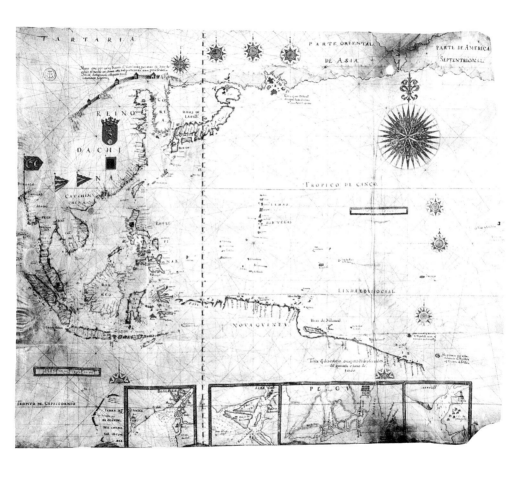

They pressed on as far as they could through the ice, but there was still no sighting of the Great Southern Continent. The men spent the winter in New Zealand and revisited Tahiti, charting nearby islands that Cook named the Friendly Islands because of the warm reception he received from the natives.

During the following year, Cook gathered data for map makers as he explored Easter Island and Tonga, New Caledonia, the New Hebrides, and the Marquesas.

On his way back to England he sailed around South Georgia. By doing so he was the first to circumnavigate an Antarctic island.

Indian Ocean
───────────

Pieter Goos, 1660
Parchment, 71.5 x 89 cm
Bibliothèque nationale de France, Paris

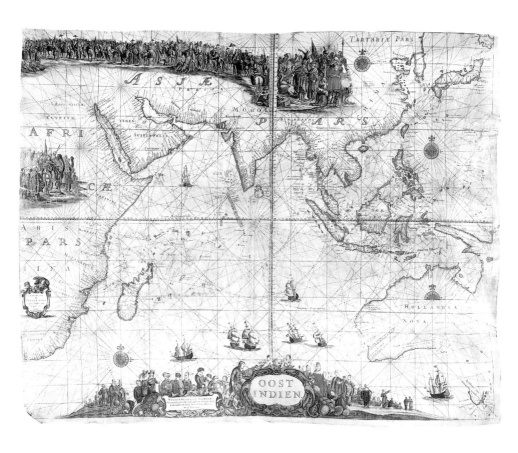

Cook's second voyage, the most famous of the three, is even more remarkable as he actually traveled not only around the world again, but actually traveled about 60,000 miles, or more than three times the circumference of the planet.

The Age of Discovery was phasing out as it overlapped with the new Age of Revolution. The French would be next with their historic revolution in 1789. The Russian, Chinese and Cuban revolutions would follow.

Four and a half months into this voyage, on December 25, Cook discovered Christmas Island, the largest atoll in the Pacific. It was not annexed to Great Britain until 1888.

The Madagascar Roadstead

Fred Woldemar, 1660
Parchment, 70.5 x 90 cm
Bibliothèque nationale de France, Paris

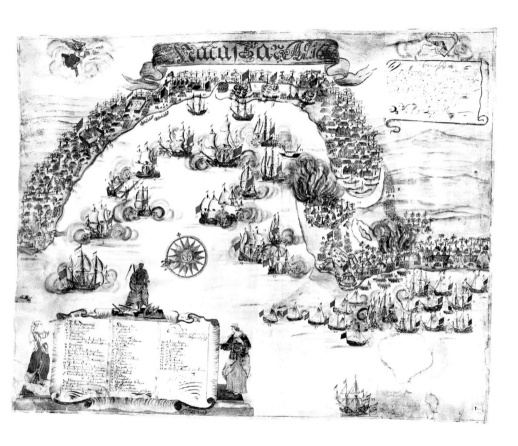

Cook then discovered the islands that he named the Sandwich Islands, after the notorious and very unpopular John Montague, 4th Earl of Sandwich who was the First Lord of the British Admiralty. The Sandwich Islands would later be renamed the Hawaiian Islands. However, it may be that Cook was not actually the first European to discover the islands.

Having delivered livestock to the island farmers, he moved on to the more important challenge of his assignment: finding a northern passage from the Pacific to the Atlantic.

Mediterranean Sea
_____

François Ollive, 1662
Parchment stuck onto one parchment sheet, 68 x 97.5 cm
Bibliothèque nationale de France, Paris

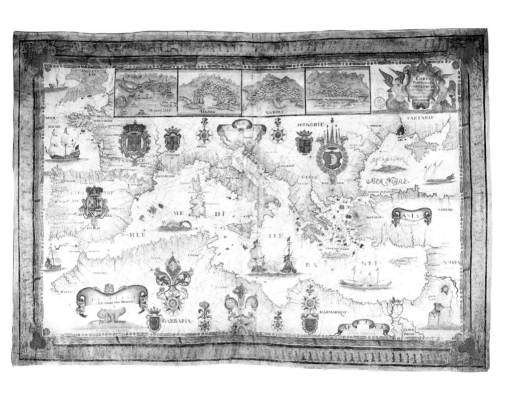

He sailed east to North America, landing at Nootka Sound, near Vancouver. Continuing up the west coast, Cook finally passed through the Bering Strait before meeting icepacks that blocked him from further advance. Still, he gathered data missing from the charts of the strait, the first charts made since those by the Danish captain, Vitus Bering, who had been to the area nearly fifty years earlier. Upon Cook's return to Hawaii, the natives made out that they considered him to be the reincarnation of one of their gods.

Indian Ocean
_____

John Burston, 1665
Parchment, 78 x 94.5 cm
Bibliothèque nationale de France, Paris

ÆGIPTVS

ARABiAFOELIX

TRO PI CVS CAN CRI

Aden

SAHID

BAR NAGASO

DOARA

MAGADOXO

ÆQVI NOC

MELINDE

QVILOA

MOSAM BIQVE

St LOKENSO

SVFF ALO

MONOMOTAPÆ

211

However, the natives then inexplicably stole one of Cook's small boats. Cook's seizure of a tribal chief as a hostage for the boat created a riot among the natives during which Cook was killed. It was an ironic end for a non violent man.

John and James Ross (John, 1777-1856)
The British Arctic explorer and rear admiral John Ross, born in Scotland in 1777, set out in search of the North West Passage in 1818. With him was his nephew, James Clark Ross, who himself also later became a rear admiral and an Arctic explorer.

The Island of Bréhat

Pierre Collin, 1666
Parchment, 96 x 75 cm
Bibliothèque nationale de France, Paris

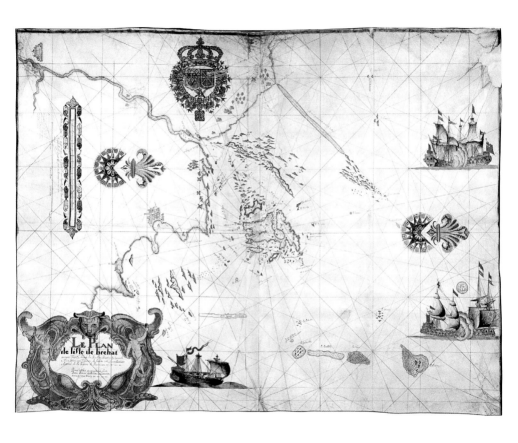

213

They reached only as far as Baffin Bay, confirming the discovery of British explorer William Baffin in 1616. Baffin had been also searching for that elusive northern waterway, but he came to believe it did not exist, a conviction that might have discouraged subsequent expeditions for some time. But neither John nor James Ross were ever put off because of previous failures. We will see that each would search for a lost expedition even though dozens of attempts had failed before.

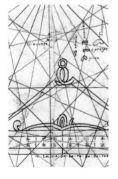

North Atlantic Ocean

Denis de Rotis, 1674
Parchment, 88 x 43.5 cm
Bibliothèque nationale de France, Paris

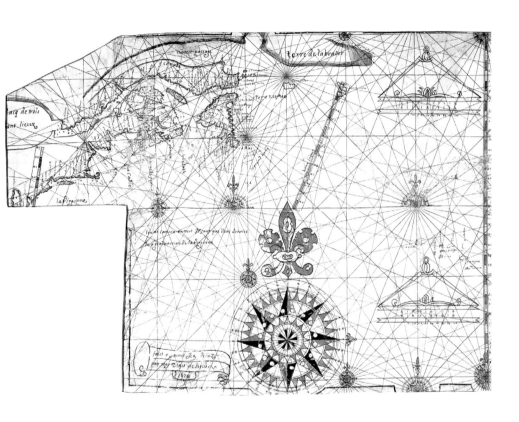

215

On a second expedition (1829-1833) with his uncle, James Ross discovered the north magnetic pole on the present Prince of Wales Island. In an age with fewer monumental discoveries, this would surely have received more notice. Meanwhile, the elder Ross discovered Boothia Peninsula and the Gulf of Boothia, both named after his financial backer, Felix Booth. John Ross also discovered King William Island – named after the British king William IV (third son of George III), whose reign began shortly after the expedition began – and explored the far north, naming Smith Sound, Jones Sound and Lancaster Sound.

The Hudson and Davis Straits

Unknown Artist, before 1677
Parchment, 40.6 x 57 cm
Bibliothèque nationale de France, Paris

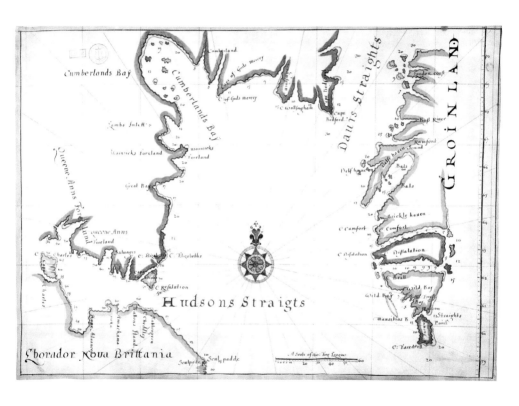

Cumberlands Bay

Cumberlands

C: of Gods mercey

C: of Gods mercey

Dauis Straights

London coast

GROIN LAND

Lumbs Inlett

Warwicks Foreland

Warwicks
Foreland

Cape
Bedford

Roß River

Ramford

Delf haven Sound

Delf haven Sound

Bala

Bala

Great Bay

Queene Anns Foreland

Queene Anns
Foreland

Brickly hauen

C: Comfort

Comfort

C: Elizabeth

C: Elizabeth

C: Desolation

Disolation

Salvages

Krill

Wild Bay

Wild Bay

C: Charles

C: Charles

C: Resolution

Manson
Bay
Manson

Mauritias B:

Straights
Point

Hudsons Straigts

C: Farewell

Chorador Nova Brittania

Churchera
Chiddly
Resolution Iland

Mare Mauricius

Seahorse

Sculpadde

A Scale of 600 Eng: Leagues

Besides sailing with his uncle, James Ross had accompanied William Parry on several voyages, and in his own expeditions to the Antarctic James Ross discovered the sea, island, and shelf ice-sheet, each to be named Ross.

John Franklin (1786-1847)

More than forty expeditions over the years searched unsuccessfully for the British explorer John Franklin and his 134 men. Eventually, between 1857 and 1859, John Rae and Francis McClintock (who had been with Franklin on an earlier expedition) determined that ships they found frozen in the ice between Victoria Island and King William Island were indeed those of Franklin.

Critical position of H.M.S. Investigator on the north-coast of Baring Island. August 20th. 1851

Samuel Gurney Cresswell, 1851
in A Series of Eight Sketches in Colour of the
Voyage of H.M.S. Investigator... London, 1854
Royal Geographical Society

Documents in metal tubes left behind by the expedition were buried under rocks and covered over with wooden markers. They told what had happened to the expedition, including the fact that Franklin had died in 1847. Other men also perished and were buried near the markers. Still others set out to travel south across the frozen surface but there are no known survivors.

Like Columbus, who died apparently convinced that he had reached the West Indies, the members of the Franklin expedition surely died thinking they had not reached the North West Passage. Ironically, they had!

The Monomotapa Empire

João Teixeira Albernas, the Younger, 1677
Parchment, 61.5 x 50 cm
Bibliothèque nationale de France, Paris

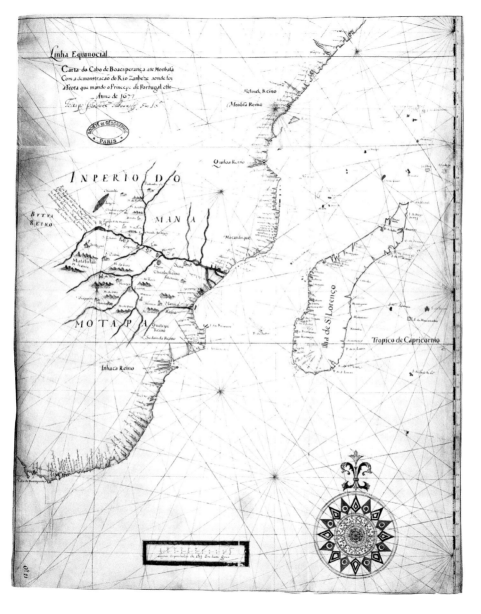

Linha Equinocial

Carta do Cabo de Boaesperança ate Monbala
Com a demonstração do Rio Zambeze aonde foi
a Frota que mando o Princepe de Portugal ette
Anno de 1677

INPERIO DO

MANIA

BYTVA REINO

Matalulus

MOTAPA

Inhaca Reino

Melinde Reino

Monbla Reino

Quiloa Reino

Maçandiquo

Ilha de S. Lorenço

Tropico de Capricornio

James Knight (1640-1719)

Tragedy struck once again when Englishman James Knight's voyage to Hudson's Bay in 1719, when Knight, in his seventies, set sail with two ships and forty men to seek the North West Passage. Like Franklin's expedition, Knight's was also lost and evidence not found for three centuries. During four seasons of investigation, Beattie and Geiger found the ship's remains submerged in the Arctic near Marble Island, known to the Inuit as 'Dead Man's Island', off the north-west coast of Hudson's Bay. No significant forensic conclusion about the fate of Knight or his sailors has been made.

Mocha

———

Augustine Fitzhugh, 1683
Parchment, 32.5 x 38.5 cm
Bibliothèque nationale de France, Paris

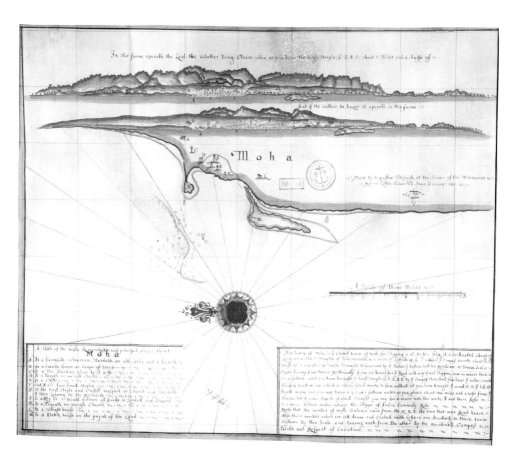

William Edward Parry (1790-1855)

In 1790, the British naval officer George Vancouver explored the North West coast of North America, from San Francisco to British Columbia. Both Vancouver Island and Vancouver, British Columbia, are named after him.

The year 1790 was also the birth year of another British naval officer and explorer, William Edward Parry. While a naval lieutenant, Parry proved himself to be a serious yet innovative scientist. After making many careful astronomical observations in the northern latitudes he published Nautical Astronomy by Night in 1816.

The Coast of North West Java

Joan Blaeu, 1688
Parchment, 41.5 x 103 cm
Bibliothèque nationale de France, Paris

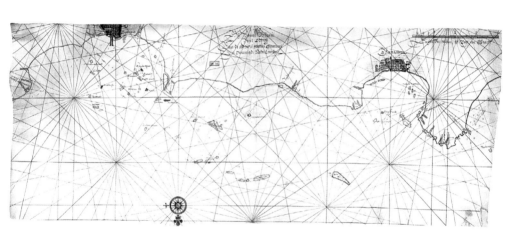

Even though he was only twenty six, his work earned respect and notice from colleagues. Participating in the Arctic expedition of explorer John Ross in 1818, Parry had command of a brig. Although that expedition was unsuccessful, the experience contributed over the next twelve months toward his obtaining the chief command of two ships for his own Arctic expedition. Later that same year Parry led a second expedition to pioneer the North West Passage, but it too failed to make it through, and he returned in 1823. When in 1827 the British finally shifted their sights from the attained practicality of reaching the

Map of the Island of Newfoundland

Pierre Detcheverry, 1689
Parchment, 57 x 31.5 cm
Bibliothèque nationale de France, Paris

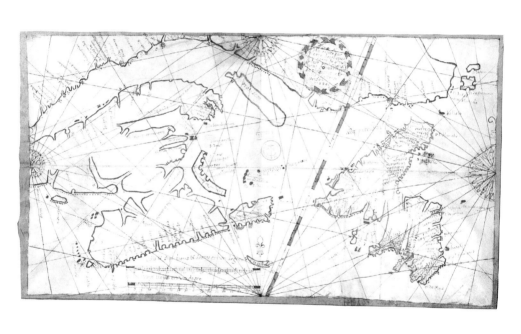

227

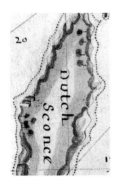

Pacific from the East to the as yet elusive glory of reaching the North Pole, Parry was commissioned to attempt a voyage to that northern extremity. While he is forever associated with endeavoring to attain that goal, ironically the most northern point Parry ever reached was in fact latitude 82° 45′ North.

Parry died in 1855. The human drive to explore and discover for 'God, Glory or Greed' lived on, for that year. Scottish missionary, physician and explorer, David Livingston discovered Victoria Falls and the Zambezi River. In 1856 he was at least the first non-African, if not the first man, to cross the continent from its west coast to the Indian Ocean.

The Banda Islands

Unknown Artist, c. 1690
Parchment, 35.5 x 54 cm
Bibliothèque nationale de France, Paris

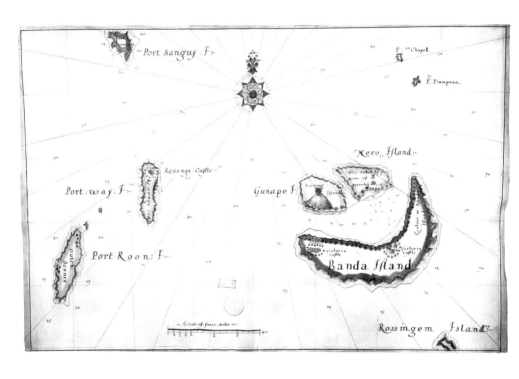

Port sanguy: I:

P. 2n Chapell

P. Prampuan

Nero Island:

Castles called by ye name of ye Iapanes nich

Revenge: Castle

Port: way: I:

Gunape I.

Burning Island

Rockes or Rising Rocke

Port: Roon: I:

Dutch Sconce

Victoria castle

Victoria Castle

Banda Island

A Scale of foure miles

Rossmgem Island:

Also that year, the United States naval officer Matthew Fontaine Maury, 'the pathfinder of the seas,' published in two volumes with four maps the first text description of deep sea oceanography, The Physical Geography of the Sea, a monumental achievement. Matthew Maury's third son, Mytton Maury, later published a revised edition of his father's most famous work.

Robert Peary (1856-1920)

A year after the publication of Maury's seminal work on oceans, Pennsylvanian Robert Peary was born. When he was thirty years old Peary became intensely interested in the Arctic. In 1886, during a decade when many adventurous people were

Persian/Arabian Gulf
***
John Thornton, 1699
Parchment, 63.5 x 74.5 cm
Bibliothèque nationale de France, Paris

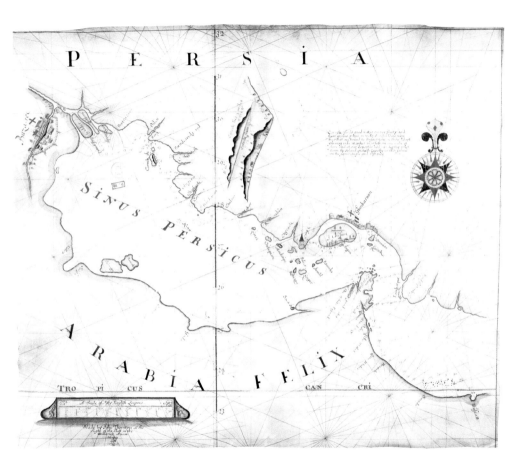

PERSIA

SINUS PERSICUS

ARABIA FELIX

TROPICUS CANCRI

A Scale of Fly English Leagues

Made by John Thornton, at the
Signe of this Hall in the
Minories, London

231

becoming more interested in inventions of electrical and mechanical things than in geographical exploration, Peary visited the interior of Greenland. Five years later he set out on one of his several scientific expeditions to the northerly part of that enormous island. Myths and superstitions about the northlands may be seen illustrated in portolani, but Peary proved that safe and economical expeditions could be made. By 1889, Peary was prepared to search for the North Pole, but, like his near-namesake Parry before him, on his early attempts he did not reach the ultimate point. At first he reached 84° 17′ North. Then, about five years later, he reached 87° 6′ North, less than 175 miles from his goal.

Amoy Bay

John Thornton, 1699
Parchment, 78 x 60.5 cm
Bibliothèque nationale de France, Paris

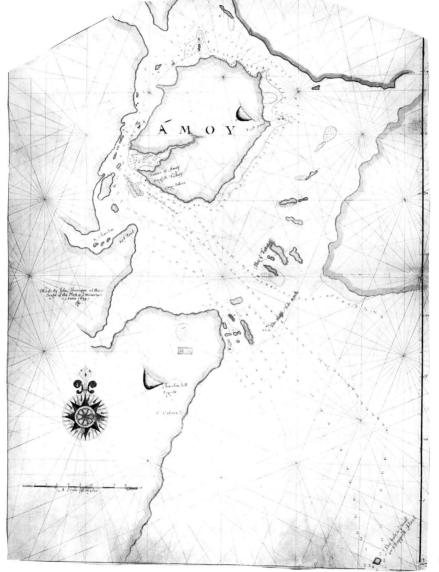

A M O Y

Made by John Thornton at the
Signe of the Platt in y.e Minories
Anno 1695

A Scale of miles

233

Finally and successfully, with a servant and four Inuit, he reached the North Pole in 1909. That same year US naturalist Roy Chapman Andrews led a scientific expedition to Alaska. Interest in the northern and southern extremes was dramatically pushing geographical exploration to its ultimate limits on the surface of the Earth. Returning to the USA from the North Pole, Peary received the disquieting news that the surgeon who had accompanied him on his 1891 expedition (F. A. Cook) had claimed that he had reached the North Pole in 1908. It took a couple years, but in 1911 Congress recognized Robert Peary's claim. Only later did scientific investigations prove his achievement.

Complete Map of All Nations

Giulio Aleni (1582-1649), c.1620

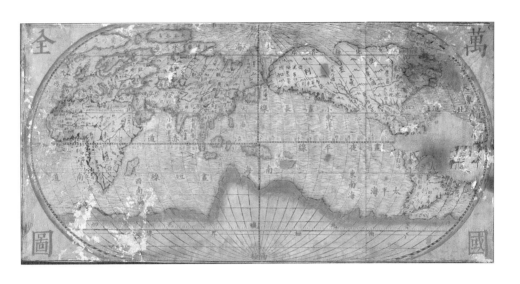

235

Roald Amundsen (1872-1928)

That same year, Norwegian Roald Amundsen was also the first man to reach the South Pole. However, his earlier achievement in 1906 was the one Europe had been working towards for centuries.

Taking three years, from 1903 to 1906, he finally broke through the many ice barriers that separated the Atlantic from the Pacific. The North West Passage was at last no longer just a theory.

Roald Amundsen

1906
Photograph
Royal Geographical Society

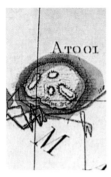

Modern Explorers: American Explorers

Once the dust settled after the American Revolutionary War (1775-1783), the next generation of Americans was eager to explore its new land and other horizons. It was as if they had to rush to catch up with centuries of discoveries and achievements already enjoyed by the rest of the world.

Looking through the list of the forty eight major American explorers who lived during the 18th and 19th centuries, we see that twenty seven of them would spend their energies on exploring the land that was, or would eventually be, their own country.

The Sandwich Islands
(later known as the Hawaiian Islands)

Rome, 1798
in Atlas of the World
Sforzesco Castle, Milan

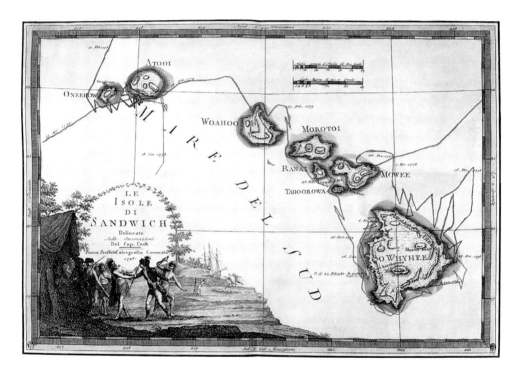

239

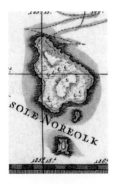

At the end of that period, ten percent (five) of them would research into and advance air exploration. And much further into the last century of the millennium, another quarter of those US explorers would be pioneers in the exploration of space.

Only ten percent (six) American explorers would continue researching into the mysteries of the oceans, continuing a process well established by older nations. American exploration began by stretching westward on land, following the Louisiana Purchase (1803).

Map of the New Hebrides
(now called Vanuatu) and New Caledonia

Rome, 1798
in Atlas of the World
Sforesco Castle, Milan

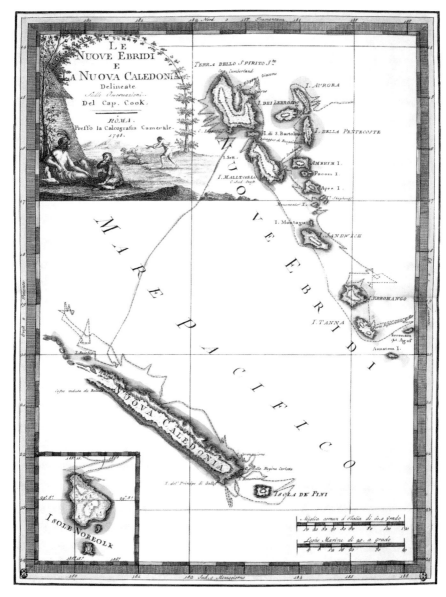

241

The boundaries were pushed still further west toward the Pacific by Lewis and Clarke (1804-1806). The adventurous men and women of the new nation were then already reaching outward by sea. From 1787 to 1790 Robert Gray captained the first US ship to circumnavigate the globe. In 1792 came the discovery of the Columbia River in Oregon (1792). Two generations later Charles Wilkes led an around-the-world expedition (1838-1842), went down into the Antarctic and discovered Wilkes Land.

Map of New Zealand

Rome, 1798
in Atlas of the World
Sforzesco Castle, Milan

As the commander of a Union warship during the US Civil War, he stopped the British mail steamer Trent and arrested two passengers who were Confederate commissioners, taking them on to Boston where they were imprisoned. Because the halting of the ship and the arrest of the men was technically piracy, the event ('the Trent Affair') became the subject of a very hasty smoothing over operation by the US and British governments of the time. The American heroes of the polar regions were men and women born only a few years after the American Revolution: Palmer and Wilkes.

Map of New Holland (Australia)
and New Guinea

———————————

Rome, 1798
in Atlas of the World
Sforzesco Castle, Milan

245

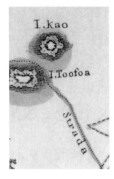

They would advance humankind's knowledge of the frozen continents during the first half of the 19th century. After them, six future American explorers of the Arctic were born late in the century. One, Robert Edwin Peary, would begin the next century by opening the frozen door even further, inspiring a dozen US explorers to continue his work well into the 1900s.

Taking up the intense interest of 19th century Europeans in exploring the polar extremes, the USA soon became a major competitor, producing some of the 20th century's greatest Arctic explorers since Palmer, Peary and Wilkes.

The Friendly Islands

Rome, 1798
in Atlas of the World
Sforzesco Castle, Milan

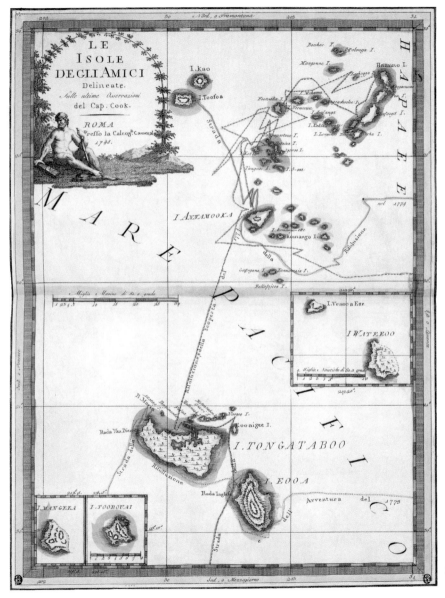

LE
ISOLE
DECLI AMICI
Delineate.
Sulle ultime Osservazioni
del Cap. Cook.

ROMA
Preſso la Calcog.a Camerale
1798.

I.Kao

I.Toofoa

Boukee I.   Ofolonga I.

Mangonne I.   Hamano I.

Fonghaego I.

Footoiha I.   I.Mehane   Hanaashooloo I.

Verncena.   Kotfanga I.

I.Lakaba   Vavaoo I. Lovaingo Tooha I.

Lapoutoua I.

Hataiva I.

Oghotero I.

Tangioa I.   O-ooa

I ANNAMOOKA

I.Komango oote
Komango I.

Gaffegana I. Yannomaia I.

Fallafapooa I.

nel 1774

Rifoluzione

Miglia Marine di 60.a grado

I.Venoo a Ette

I WATEEOO

Miglia Inutiche di 60.a grado

M.Mooa   Ndoogo I.

Rada Van Diemen   Loonigee I.

I.TONGATABOO

I. EOOA

Rada Ingleſe

Avventura   del 1775

J.MANGEIA   I.TOOBOUAI

MARE   PACIFICO

N'rd, o Tramontana

Sud, o Mezzogiorno

H A P A E E

Index

M

W